Gay & Lesbian Rights:

A Guide for GLBT Singles, Couples and Families

Other books in the *Rights* series:

Teen Rights
by Traci Truly

Unmarried Parents' Rights, 2E
by Jacqueline D. Stanley

Gay & Lesbian Rights:

A Guide for GLBT Singles, Couples and Families

Brette McWhorter Sember
Attorney at Law

SPHINX® PUBLISHING
AN IMPRINT OF SOURCEBOOKS, INC.®
NAPERVILLE, ILLINOIS
www.SphinxLegal.com

First Edition, 2003

Published by: **Sphinx® Publishing, An Imprint of Sourcebooks, Inc.®**

Naperville Office
P.O. Box 4410
Naperville, Illinois 60567-4410
630-961-3900
Fax: 630-961-2168
www.sourcebooks.com
www.SphinxLegal.com

This publication is designed to provide accurate and authoritative information in regard to the subject matter covered. It is sold with the understanding that the publisher is not engaged in rendering legal, accounting, or other professional service. If legal advice or other expert assistance is required, the services of a competent professional person should be sought.

From a Declaration of Principles Jointly Adopted by a Committee of the American Bar Association and a Committee of Publishers and Associations

This product is not a substitute for legal advice.

Disclaimer required by Texas statutes.

Library of Congress Cataloging-in-Publication Data
Sember, Brette McWhorter, 1968-
  Gay and lesbian rights : a guide for GLBT singles, couples, and families / Brette McWhorter Sember.-- 1st ed.
    p. cm.
  ISBN 1-57248-331-8 (pbk. : alk. paper)
  1. Homosexuality--Law and legislation--United States. 2. Lesbians--Civil rights--United States. 3. Gay men--Civil rights--United States. I. Title.

KF4754.5.S455 2003
342.73'085--dc21
                                                         2003005522

Printed and bound in the United States of America.

BG Paperback — 10 9 8 7 6 5 4 3 2 1

CONTENTS

DEDICATION

In memory of Gary Jackson

ACKNOWLEDGEMENTS

This book would not have been possible without the assistance and support of Donna Bugdin, owner of the Alternative Phone Book in western New York.

I would also like to thank Dr. Martin Kantor, author of *My Guy: A Gay Man's Guide to a Lasting Relationship*, for his time and valuable input.

PREFACE

This is an exciting time of change for the GLBT community. While there is more and more acceptance of the GLBT lifestyle, particularly because of celebrity openness, there are also more and more changes in the law, acknowledging gay rights and concerns. With the important new domestic partnership law in Vermont, as well as changes in Canada and California, gay couples and families are gaining more legal rights and more options.

This book is your guide to those rights and is designed to help you consider your options. Legal issues you may encounter in various aspects of your life—from employment to housing to partnership agreements to estate planning to children are addressed in this handbook. Not only does this title identify your current rights, but it also gives practical solutions for dealing with problems and concerns.

Written for GLBT singles, couples, and families, the book takes a comprehensive approach in addressing every type of legal concern that can arise. The book is designed to be a guide you can keep on your bookcase and pick up when a question or problem arises.

INTRODUCTION

This book is a roadmap to your rights as a member of the GLBT community, whether you are single, part of a couple, or a family.

Chapter 1 discusses the state of gay rights in the U.S. and offers information about what changes can be made. Chapter 2 explains the rights in various states to be free of discrimination based on sexual orientation. Your rights as you rent or purchase a home, including information about roommates and home sharing are discussed in Chapter 3.

Chapter 4 provides information about sharing bank accounts and credit cards and organizing your finances as a couple. Chapter 5 takes an important look at health insurance issues, COBRA, decision making for partners, health care directives, and end of life issues. Domestic partnership benefits, insurance issues, immigration, domestic violence and retirement issues are covered in Chapter 6.

Chapter 7 takes a close look at how to form a domestic partnership, how to modify a domestic partnership agreement and how to register a domestic partnership. California's law is discussed in detail. The laws regarding Vermont civil unions—how to get one and how to end one—are explained in Chapter 8. Chapter 9 discusses name change issues, as well as important transgender (TG) issues and concerns.

Chapter 10 deals with estate planning, wills, guardianship, powers of attorney and living trusts to protect yourself, your assets, and your partner or family. The many ways GLBT community members can become parents, from step parenting and foster care to adoption and insemination or surrogacy are addressed in Chapter 11.

Chapter 12 discusses issues important to GLBT parents—role models, discrimination, safe schools and support organizations. How to deal with parenting issues after a break up is also discussed. Chapter 13 deals with ending a relationship and explains how to enforce a domestic partnership agreement, divide belongings, seek support or palimony and get legal help. Your rights in a traditional marriage are considered in Chapter 14.

Forms are included at the end of the book. Feel free to photocopy them (enlarging them to 8 1/2" x 11"). Keep a blank original for future use or if you make a mistake completing a form. In addition, the book contains several appendices which show the text of important laws and also provides many resources to find more information.

–1–
GAY IN THE U.S.A.

In recent years there have been gradual changes in the law, slowly acknowledging, and beginning to accommodate members of the Gay, Lesbian, Bi-Sexual, and Transgender (GLBT) community. Change, however, is never fast enough. While there are adoption rights, civil unions in one state, and benefits from some employers, the changes have not been far-reaching enough to allow gays *equal* rights.

SODOMY STATUTES

The most common and blatantly anti-gay types of laws are sodomy statutes. Sodomy laws prohibit anal and sometimes oral intercourse (the laws vary by state) and make these private acts a crime. There is a perception among many straight people that these laws are not enforced or are only enforced in cases of forcible sodomy (as part of a rape or sexual assault). In fact, these laws are sometimes invoked against consenting adults (such as part of a police operation to stop solicitation) and have the effect of branding consenting adult sexual behavior as criminal and encouraging anti-gay discrimination. Enforcement of the laws has also been used as evidence to support employment discrimination and discrimination in custody proceedings.

Furthermore, those convicted of sodomy are considered *sex crime offenders* and have to comply with state sex offender registries (often known as *Megan's Law*) and community notification. They also often feel as if their privacy has been completely violated and must deal with resulting feelings of anger, guilt, and resentment.

These laws stand as a clear sign to the GLBT community that they are not accepted by the straight establishment.

Sodomy laws impose fines or jail terms of up to twenty years upon conviction, making them not only laws of prejudice, but also laws of great injustice. In 1986, the United States Supreme Court in *Bowers v. Hardwick* upheld Georgia's law against sodomy and decided that there is no fundamental right to engage in consensual homosexual sodomy and that the right to privacy does not include the right to engage in this activity. This ruling still stands, but a new pending Supreme Court case from Texas will test the Texas law. *Lawrence and Garner v. Texas* challenges the Texas sodomy law used to convict two men who engaged in consensual sodomy in the privacy of one of their homes.

States that have specific laws against consensual sodomy between same sex partners are:

◆ Kansas;
◆ Missouri (The law remains in effect, but a 1999 case held it does not apply to consensual relations. It continues to be used in some jurisdictions in Missouri.);
◆ Oklahoma; and,
◆ Texas (Currently prohibited in Texas, the law will be considered by the United States Supreme Court in *Lawrence and Garner v. Texas*. Read more about this case at **www.lambdalegal.org**).

States that prohibit consensual sodomy between same sex and opposite sex couples are:

◆ Alabama;
◆ Florida;
◆ Idaho;
◆ Louisiana;
◆ Mississippi;
◆ North Carolina;
◆ South Carolina;
◆ Utah; and,
◆ Virginia.

CHANGING THE LAWS

Throughout this book we will look at the state of the current laws and how they impact your life. You probably will not agree with the way many laws are written (since there are not too many that are pro-gay) and proba-

RAINBOW TIP

Read SpeakOut.com's list of ten gay activism tips to help get your message out:

speakout.com/activism/tips

bly will feel that gays are often treated as second class citizens.

We can work to change this. Get involved on the local level with area pride organizations. Become a member of state and national pride and gay activist organizations (check the resource appendix for more information). Contact your state and federal representatives with your concerns about how your rights are being violated. Ask family members and friends to do the same. Things can only change if gay voices are heard and if public awareness is increased.

SUPPORTING THE COMMUNITY

Another way to increase awareness and stand for gay rights is to actively support your local gay community. Many communities have gay phone books, often referred to as the *Alternative Phone Book*, *Lavender Phone Book*, or *Pink Pages*, that list businesses that support gays. Seek out businesses, service providers, and suppliers who support the GLBT community. In some communities, businesses will display rainbow stickers on their doors or windows as a signal that they are *gay friendly*. Check **www.rainbowquery.com** for local pride contact information.

When you support businesses that support the community, you add resources to the GLBT community. You show other businesses that they are missing out on the economic benefit the gay community can provide.

Gay communities can have a powerful economic impact simply by choosing to patronize businesses that support the GLBT community. Advertising and media specialists are just beginning to understand the power of "DINK" (Double Income, No Kids—which is often an accurate way to describe gay couples). Use your resources to support your community and refuse to work with merchants who will not support it. Look for your local gay phone book, seek out local or regional gay magazines or newspapers and patronize the advertisers. In Britain, the financial effect of the GLBT community is called the "pink pound."

VOTING WITH YOUR FEET

"Voting with your feet" is an old saying that means if your vote does not count, pick up and move to where it does. For example, since Vermont passed the civil union law, many gay couples have chosen to move to Vermont or at the very least, visited there to take advantage of the law.

Voting with your feet is a choice you have. However it is important to remember that you should not have to pick up and move because politicians in your local area have failed to recognize your rights. You should have access to equal rights wherever you live. Many gay couples do prefer to move to a locale where they feel more accepted. They often choose to first find personal comfort and then work to change laws throughout the rest of the country.

Canada is becoming an option for more and more people, as there are rapid changes happening there with regard to gay rights. Recently, the Ontario Superior Court ruled that marriage could include same sex couples, but suspended the ruling for two years to give the Canadian federal government time to rephrase its definition of marriage. The issue is far from decided, but steps have been taken in the right direction.

GETTING LEGAL HELP

Although this book is designed to give you the information you need to solve a lot of problems on your own, you may at some point find yourself in a situation where you need an attorney. Situations such as adoption, discrimination lawsuits, probate of wills, dissolution of civil unions, and contested division of property after a break up will probably require an attorney. If you have an attorney that you have used for other matters, talk to him or her about the current situation. Find out if he or she can recommend another attorney qualified to handle this matter if he or she is not.

Lambda Legal is an organization dedicated to handling gay and lesbian cases, but you may find that the organization can help you only if your case will be an important one—one that sets new standards. You can however contact their regional offices to see if they can provide you with a list of attorneys in your area to contact. The same holds true for the ACLU (American Civil Liberties Union). These and other GLBT resources are included in Appendix E.

To find legal help in your area, talk to local pride leaders and if your area has a gay phone book check there. Word of mouth is a good way to find an attorney who is experienced in handling cases that involve gay issues. If you are unable to find an attorney in this way, you can contact your local or state bar association for a referral to an attorney experienced in handling your type of case. If you do call for a referral, make it clear that you are specifically looking for a gay-friendly attorney.

If you cannot afford an attorney, contact your local legal aid office and find out if they will accept your case. In addition, many bar associations have volunteer lawyers programs. Your local bar association can offer information about this.

When you meet with an attorney, ask point blank if he or she is comfortable working with a gay client and if he or she can handle your case with enthusiasm. You have every right to find an attorney who supports and respects you.

–2–
PROTECTION FROM DISCRIMINATION

Unfortunately, discrimination is still a problem for the GLBT community. Understanding your rights is your first line of defense and encouraging your state and federal representatives to introduce and support legislation preventing discrimination based upon sexual orientation is the way to make changes happen.

WHAT IS DISCRIMINATION?

Discrimination occurs when you are treated differently than other people because you are gay, lesbian, bisexual or transgender/transsexual. Any time someone treats you differently because of this, it is discrimination. However, legal protection exists only in certain circumstances.

Discrimination with No Recourse

Jacques and Wil walk into a restaurant holding hands. The hostess gives them a shocked look and asks them to wait a few minutes for a table. As they wait, they notice other people coming in and being seated. After ten minutes, Wil asks when their table will be ready. The hostess tells him they are quite backed up and it will be a few minutes more. They decide to wait. They are finally seated in the rear corner of the restaurant. The server is unfriendly and forgets to bring them napkins, doesn't fill up their water glasses, and doesn't stop by to check how their food is. Other servers stare at them as they are eating. They leave the restaurant feeling distinctly unwelcome.

Discrimination with legal recourse (in some states)
Suzanne and Brandy are looking for an apartment where they can live with their 4 year old son. They go to see an apartment with their son along one day. While the landlord is showing them the apartment, their son refers to one of them as "Mommy" and the other as "Mama." The landlord asks, "What, are you gay or something?" They respond that they are. He immediately shows them out and tells them he does not rent to *their kind*.

To determine whether you have been legally discriminated against, you need to understand what specific protections your state offers and determine if your rights have been violated under those laws.

FEDERAL PROTECTION
There is no federal law that prevents or punishes discrimination on the basis of sexual orientation. While there are laws that prevent discrimination based on sex, this does not offer protection based on sexual orientation.

The *Federal Fair Housing Act* does prohibit housing discrimination based on HIV status (defined as a "handicap" under the law), thus you cannot be denied a rental because you are HIV positive or have AIDS.

STATE LAW PROTECTIONS

Where the federal government has failed to act, many states have stepped in and enacted laws offering protection against discrimination. These are discussed in detail later in the chapter. Many municipalities and counties have enacted local laws prohibiting this kind of discrimination. For a list of these current municipalities, see **www.lambdalegal.org/cgi-bin/iowa/documents/record?record=217.**

If you have been the victim of discrimination and your state offers protection, contact your state human rights department or the state attorney general for information on how to file a complaint or bring a lawsuit. You can also contact Lambda Legal at **www.lambdalegal.org** or 212-809-8585 or contact any of the other GLBT legal organizations listed in Appendix E.

If your state does not offer protection, contact your state senator and state representative to express the need for such a law. If you have been discriminated against and your state does not offer protection, you may still be protected if some other basis for discrimination was present, such as sex, age, or national origin.

> ## RAINBOW TIP
>
> Information to record in case of housing discrimination:
> • the ad you responded to;
> • address of the property;
> • name of landlord and/or person who showed you the unit;
> • dates you viewed the unit;
> • notes about questions you were asked at the time;
> • notes about who was with you when you viewed the unit; and,
> • information you shared about yourself.

In the following sections, we will look at the specific types of protections offered by various states. These laws can be found on your state legislature's or attorney general's web sites and also at **www.findlaw.com**. You can also find a list of state by state GLBT discrimination cases at **www.buddybuddy.com/d-p-ngl.html**.

Housing Discrimination

Housing discrimination occurs when a GLBT person is denied housing or is held to different standards or requirements—such as higher rent, a larger security deposit, or a rule about no overnight guests.

While the federal government does not offer protection from housing discrimination based on sexual orientation, the following states do:

◆ Connecticut;
◆ Hawaii;
◆ Maryland;
◆ Massachusetts;
◆ Minnesota;
◆ New Hampshire;
◆ New Jersey;
◆ Rhode Island;
◆ Vermont;
◆ Washington D.C.; and,
◆ Wisconsin.

NOTE: *Connecticut, Minnesota, and Rhode Island also extend protection to TG individuals.*

If you experience housing discrimination in one of these states, contact your state's housing department to report the incident. If your state does not offer protection, you should still contact your state's housing department and make it clear that this form of discrimination is happening. Only by making people aware can things be changed.

Not all housing discrimination occurs at the time you attempt rent a unit. Sometimes a landlord learns or figures out that tenants are gay and attempts to terminate the lease. A lease can only be terminated for the reasons listed in it. Usually these reasons include nonpayment, creating a nuisance (being gay is NOT a nuisance), or violating one of the terms of the lease. If your state has anti-sodomy laws, being gay can possibly be used as a reason (since the landlord can say you are committing an illegal act).

If you do not have a lease and your agreement is month-to-month it means that either you or your landlord can decide to end the lease with one month's notice. The landlord does not have to give you a reason for this. Even if he or she tells you it is because you are gay, you do not have much recourse, unless your state prohibits housing discrimination.

Credit Discrimination
Credit discrimination can include being denied credit, being subjected to additional scrutiny, higher interest rates, or different terms. The *Federal Equal Opportunity Credit Act* does not prohibit discrimination based on sexual orientation. The following states have laws that do prohibit this:

- Connecticut;
- Massachusetts;
- Minnesota;
- Rhode Island;
- Vermont;
- Washington, D.C.; and,
- Wisconsin.

If you have experienced credit discrimination in a state where there is protection, contact the state attorney general's office or state consumer protection agency. If your state does not offer protection, it is a good idea to still report it to one of these state agencies. Only patronize banks and financial institutions that do not discriminate on the basis of sexual orientation.

Employment Discrimination
Employment discrimination happens when a person is not hired, is fired, or is held to different standards or requirements while on the job because he or she is a member of the GLBT community. It can include being denied promotions or pay increases, being subjected to different standards or requirements, and being treated in a hostile or unfriendly manner. These states prohibit discrimination based on sexual orientation in *public employment*:

- Illinois;
- Iowa;
- Maryland;
- New Mexico;
- Pennsylvania; and,
- Washington.

Discrimination is prohibited in both *public and private employment* based sexual orientation in the following states:
- California;
- Connecticut;
- Hawaii;
- Massachusetts;
- Minnesota;
- Nevada;
- New Hampshire;
- New Jersey;
- New York;
- Rhode Island;
- Vermont;
- Washington, D.C.; and,
- Wisconsin.

Additionally there may be county or local laws that prohibit discrimination in your area. Many companies have also adopted company policies prohibiting discrimination. Check with your human resources department about your company's policy.

If you are not protected by state or local laws, you can still sue an employer for emotional distress, harassment, defamation (saying bad things about you that damage your reputation) and wrongful termination (if you were fired just because you were gay and there was no other reason). It is important to talk with an employment law attorney who can help you put together a good case. Be sure to keep careful records of incidents and situations to help prove your case.

The Supreme Court recently held in *Chevron U.S.A. vs. Eschazabal* that employers can turn down applicants if they feel the job could endanger their health. Be aware that this may be used as a reason to turn down HIV-positive applicants. Additionally, there are some states that require HIV testing as a prerequisite to obtaining certain licenses (such as a massage therapist license for example). These restrictions may be in violation of the *Americans With Disabilities Act*. If you find yourself in this position, get an attorney.

RAINBOW TIP

Read the current *Human Rights Campaign Corporate Equality Index Survey* (an evaluation of which companies are GLBT friendly) at:
www.hrc.org/worknet/index.asp

Transgender Employment Discrimination

TG employees often encounter difficult situations at work when they begin to dress in clothing of the opposite sex. Employers have the right to require dress codes or set basic requirements for employee clothing. These rules must be applied evenly across the board to all employees in similar positions. Employers can require different types of clothing for men and women. Difficulties arise when a person begins to dress as the opposite sex as part of a transgender program or as a personal choice. Employers can require people to follow codes of dress for their gender. Many employers are willing to allow a transgendering individual to switch clothing before the actual gender change, but often documentation or contact from doctors or therapists is necessary to gain cooperation.

Another issue is that of rest rooms. Once a person adopts the dress of the other gender, he or she will wish to use the corresponding restroom. Some employers have unisex or handicap bathrooms that can be used by anyone. For facilities that do not, this can pose problems for other workers who are uncomfortable sharing a restroom with a person who is transitioning. Lambda Legal Services recommends that transgendering individuals place a sign on the restroom indicating that he or she is in the currently in the restroom, to alert those who may be uncomfortable. Employers can limit restroom usage by gender, but OSHA (Occupational Safety and Health Administration) requires that all employees have access to a convenient restroom while working, so you have an absolute right to have a restroom you can use. At least one case has held that employers can tell employees to use a restroom that matches their appearance, and other employees using that restroom who complain can be offered a different one for their use. See Chapter 9 for more information about TG issues.

RAINBOW TIP

For assistance with TG legal issues, contact:

> National Transgender
> Advocacy Coalition
> 14252 Culver Drive, #904
> Irvine, California 92604-0326
> www.ntac.org

For human rights laws addressing TGs, visit the Transgender Law & Policy Institute at:

> www.transgenderlaw.org

School Discrimination

Nine states have Safe School Laws, that prohibit discrimination based on sexual orientation. They include:

- ◆ California;
- ◆ Connecticut;
- ◆ Massachusetts;
- ◆ Minnesota;
- ◆ New Jersey;
- ◆ Vermont;
- ◆ Washington;
- ◆ Washington, D.C.; and,
- ◆ Wisconsin.

Only four states prohibit discrimination in schools based on gender identity:

- ◆ California;
- ◆ Minnesota;

- New Jersey; and,
- Washington, D.C.

Many public schools have developed safe school programs for children of GLBT families and for gay teens. See Chapter 12 for more information about these programs.

RAINBOW TIP

For a list of GLBT Greek organizations, visit:
www.bglad.com/education_and_
learning/fraternities_and_sororities

Many colleges and universities have instituted anti-discrimination policies. If you or your child are planning to attend a college or university, find out what the school's policy is. Check for conduct codes, anti-discrimination policies, and anti-harassment policies. Find out if your school has any gay Greek organizations, gay student organizations, or support and/or resource center for GLBT students.

HATE CRIME LAWS

Hate crimes are crimes against people or property committed because of the victim's race, sexual orientation, ethnicity, religion or other minority status. The *Matthew Shepard* case brought a lot of media attention to these crimes.

Twenty-four states have hate crime laws that specifically mention sexual orientation. These states are:

- California;
- Connecticut;
- Delaware;
- Florida;
- Hawaii;
- Illinois;
- Kentucky;
- Louisiana;
- Maine;
- Massachusetts;
- Minnesota;
- Missouri;

- ◆ Nebraska;
- ◆ Nevada;
- ◆ New Hampshire;
- ◆ New Jersey;
- ◆ New York;
- ◆ Oregon;
- ◆ Rhode Island;
- ◆ Vermont;
- ◆ Washington;
- ◆ Washington D.C.; and,
- ◆ Wisconsin.

Arizona, Montana, Maryland, and Utah have hate crime laws, but they do not impose penalties for those based on sexual orientation, however they do collect data on these crimes. California, Minnesota, Michigan, Missouri, Pennsylvania, Vermont and Washington D.C. have hate crime laws that punish based on gender identity.

In general, these laws provide punishment in addition to the penalties that would normally apply to the specific act of violence when crimes are committed out of hate.

There is great debate about hate crime legislation. Many people feel that these laws are important in stopping the spread of bigotry and in making people aware that it is wrong to act out in hate against someone simply because of who he or she is. Other people believe that these laws are a way to limit freedom of thought and to single out people for extra protection who hold beliefs that are contrary to those held by most Americans.

In 2000, Congress passed the federal *Local Law Enforcement Enhancement Act* (which was formerly called the *Hate Crime Prevention Act*), which gave the federal government expanded ability to assist and intervene in cases involving hate crimes. It expanded the protection to include sexual orientation.

If you or someone you know is the victim of a crime that you believe is motivated by bias, your first step is to talk to the local police. Tell them you want to file a complaint under your state's hate crime law and/or under the federal hate crimes law. If local law enforcement does not take you seriously, call your state attorney general and get in touch with local or national gay activist groups which can provide legal assistance. (See Appendix E for additional resources.)

DISCRIMINATION IN THE MILITARY

The U.S. military has a long standing aversion to homosexuals. This was supposed to turn around with the passage of the 1993 Executive Order signed by President Clinton, enacting the *don't ask, don't tell* policy. This policy is still in effect and prohibits the military from asking if an applicant or service person is gay. It prohibits harassment against those service people believed or suspected to be gay. However, if a service person discloses that he or she is gay, he or she will be discharged.

This policy was upheld by the Fourth Circuit Court of Appeals in *Thomasson v. Perry* in 1996. Earlier, in 1995, another Executive Order was signed removing sexual orientation as a basis for denying a person security clearance.

Despite these new regulations, discrimination against gays in the military continues with harassment, fear, and non-acceptance creating a cold climate. In 2001, 1250 service personnel were discharged on the basis of being homosexual. The number of discharges continues to grow every year. Improper investigations continue to proliferate—such as disclosures from therapists of confidential information. Females who report sexual harassment are often retaliated against with allegations of being gay. Aside from the obvious violations of privacy and unnecessary discharges, the problem with the policy is that it sends mixed messages. It fails to fully support the rights of gays to serve in the military. (See Appendix E for support organizations for gays in the military.)

RAINBOW TIP

Tips for getting help with discrimination problems:

- report the incident to the state agency that deals with the situation in which it has occurred;
- report the incident in writing and keep a copy;
- follow up on your complaint and keep a record of your phone conversations and contacts;
- contact local GLBT pride and advocacy organizations for assistance and support; and,
- if you have no legal protection in your area, write to your state representatives about your situation and the lack of legal protection.

DISCRIMINATION BY PRIVATE ORGANIZATIONS

When the Boy Scouts refused to allow gays to be troop leaders and this refusal was upheld by the U.S. Supreme Court in *Boy Scouts of America v. Dale*, it became clear that legal protection against discrimination by private organizations is not forthcoming. At this point, advocacy is the only way to change opinions and open minds.

–3–
HOME SWEET HOME

The time has come for your first (or next) apartment, or maybe you are looking to buy. Maybe you are thinking about moving in with your partner. When it comes to living arrangements, members of the GLBT community face some unique considerations. Renting can result in difficult situations if sexual orientation is an issue for the landlord. Buying a home involves complicated paperwork and financial decision-making. Both of these situations become even more complicated if you and your partner decide to live together. This chapter will discuss some of the issues surrounding home renting and buying.

RENTING
Discrimination is a real problem with some landlords. In most places across the U.S. (see Chapter 2 for more details), there are no laws preventing housing discrimination against homosexuals. This means that there is very little legal protection. Besides the stress of needing a place to live, dealing with housing discrimination can be very emotional. It is insulting, stressful, and upsetting. It is important to know your options.

Potential Landlords
One option you have is to not reveal your personal life to prospective or current landlords. If asked, you can lie or be circumspect. Your partner is your roommate, after all. You do not need to come out and announce *we're gay*. Many gay rights activists will point out, however, that this answer is not going to help to change people's

misconceptions. You are free to tell a potential landlord anything you want about your personal life. This is the best way to get it all out up front and avoid an even more frustrating situation in an eviction action.

You can refuse to rent from someone who is bigoted. Hitting them in their wallet may lead to some sort of tolerance in certain circumstances. Sometimes though you have to make a choice based on personal needs and not on ideals. Balancing these two is a choice each individual must make for her or himself.

If you are fortunate to live in state that offers housing discrimination protection and you are denied housing because you are GLBT, you need to contact your state attorney general's office, state human rights agency, or state housing department. In order to prove the discrimination occurred because of your sexual or gender identity, you need to be able to give actual proof—for example, a statement by the landlord or a showing that straight applicants who were less qualified were rented to instead of you. If you win your case you may be entitled to expenses (such as moving and storage fees), attorney's fees, and other expenses you incurred.

Current Landlord

While you do not have many options if you are denied housing from a prospective landlord (unless you are lucky enough to live in a state where this is prohibited), you are in a different position with an existing landlord. If you have a lease, your landlord cannot simply decide to evict you because he or she discovers or suspects you are gay. You can only be evicted for reasons stated in the lease and for nonpayment. Of course, landlords have been known to try to find excuses to evict gay tenants. If this happens to you, be very vocal about what is happening. Make it clear to the housing court judge that you are being targeted because of your sexuality. Keep careful records of the problems you encounter.

If you are a month to month tenant (in other words, you have no written lease), your landlord can decide not to renew with one month's notice. There is not much you can do about this situation, since you have no lease and no guarantee beyond a month. Even if your state offers no protection, many municipalities have laws prohibiting housing discrimination against gays. Check your local laws or talk to gay activists in your area for more information about your rights under local law.

If you are being evicted because you are gay, usually the landlord will come up with another reason for the eviction. You will need to prove that this reason (nonpayment, noisiness, extensive damage) is not true. Respond in court and bring evidence that supports your argument.

Roommate Agreements

While co-habitating heterosexuals can face similar problems, gay couples deciding to move in together may face additional resistance from landlords. Many leases require that notice be given to your landlord before adding a roommate, and that the landlord must approve of the new person. While this may be as simple as a credit check to satisfy the landlord's desire to protect his or her investment, it can be used to keep your partner out, or to get rid of you if you violate the lease terms.

If you move in together but do not formally tell the landlord, in addition to possibly violating your lease, you might be violating a notification law—some states require that tenants notify a landlord if they add a roommate. If the new roommate is known to the landlord, then his or her consent is implied. The roommate can become a tenant if he or she pays rent to the landlord (for example, you each pay half the rent directly to the landlord). If he or she accepts it, then consent is implied.

> **RAINBOW TIP**
>
> Before moving in with a partner, it is a good idea to get a sense for the other person's habits, cleanliness, and hours. Living with someone is hard work. You can lay down some basic rules that will make it easier for both of you. Try this roommate compatibility test:
>
> www.hiram.edu/wizard_roommate /roomate_wiz.asp

After passing the notification hurdle, some partners prefer to change the lease so both partners are listed. You will be able to add your partner to the lease only if the landlord agrees. Doing this is an important decision, because should you break up, you cannot simply tell your roommate to get out. He or she will have a legal right to remain in the unit. Also, remember that when both of your names are on the lease, you are both responsible for the rent. For example, if your partner loses his or her job and has no income, you will be held responsible by the landlord for the entire rent if your partner does not pay his or her portion.

For this reason, it is often better to have a roommate agreement when one party is initially moving into the residence of the other. If you choose to become life partners, you can at that point discuss modifying the lease to add the roommate's name to it or go out and rent a new apartment together.

The decision to live together is an important step. Because it is so significant emotionally, it is a good idea to be clear about how you will share expenses and space. Use the Roommate Agreement (form 3, p.230) to do this. Before moving in together, you need to have a clear understanding as to what expenses you each will be responsible for.

Some samples of expense sharing agreements include:

- ◆ Each partner will pay one half of the rent and utility bills;
- ◆ Partner A will pay the water and cable bill, Partner B will pay the electric and gas bill, both partners will pay half of the non-itemized phone bill and will pay portions of the itemized phone bill that each is responsible for;
- ◆ Partner A will pay all of the rent and Partner B will pay all utility bills. Grocery expenses will be shared evenly;
- ◆ Each partner will pay expenses in proportion to his or her income (total your incomes and then divide your individual income by the total to find out what your percent of the total income is. You would then pay that percent of all expenses; or,
- ◆ Partner A will pay 25% of the rent, half of all utility bills and all of the grocery expenses. Partner B will pay 75% of the rent.

It is important to remember that if you are entering a life partnership, that the rent and utility expenses will be just part of your entire expense sharing plan. When you decide to enter a life partnership, it makes more sense to create an all-encompassing Domestic Partnership Agreement. For more information, see Chapter 7. Also see Appendix F for a copy of a sample Domestic Partnership Agreement.

When first moving in together you also want to be clear on how the apartment will be shared. Will you each have a closet? Will you each have part of a room for a home office? Will the partner moving in bring his or her furniture and fit it into the apartment? It is best to discuss these types of plans in advance so you do not run into a situation where suddenly the partner moving in clears out half of a closet to make room for his or her things, or expects to be able to put his or her large screen tv in a tiny bedroom. While there are legal ramifications to this new living arrangement, the emotion, stress, and impact may be the greater concern.

OWNING

Owning a home on your own is a wonderful kind of responsibility. If buying a home on your own, you may encounter some discrimination, but it is not as likely as if you are purchasing a home with a partner (see below). Your state laws about credit discrimination will apply to mortgages, so make sure you are aware of your rights. (see Chapter 2.)

Buying a Home Together

Purchasing a home together is an exciting step. You will want to meet with a mortgage banker prior to finding the home of your dreams to get an idea of what size mortgage your incomes will qualify you for. Again, there are no laws protecting you

RAINBOW TIP

For a referral to a GLBT friendly real estate professional, visit:
http://homelounge.com

from discrimination while seeking credit. If you meet resistance from one banker, find another. You have money to spend and there are bankers out there who want it.

Find a real estate broker or agent you are comfortable with and start your house hunt. Though very rare, there are some places where you might encounter discriminatory zoning regulations prohibiting people who are not related from living together in the neighborhood. It is important to find out about this before making an offer on a home, so check with your real estate agent.

Once you find a home and decide to purchase it, you want to make sure that you purchase it as *joint tenants with right of survivorship*, which means that you will each own the home together in equal shares. This wording is specific and needs to be stated on the deed. In some states, *joint tenancy* means the same thing, but make sure you verify this. The seller's attorney generally prepares the deed, so it is important he or she is informed as to how the ownership is to be described.

Joint tenancy also means that if one of you dies, the other will own the home. This can be a vital protection as the property will pass to the joint owner apart from your state's inheritance rights. Neither one of you can pass ownership in this property through your will if it is jointly owned. Jointly owned property passes *outside of probate*. This applies to real property such as your home, as well as personal property, such as a joint checking account.

Another ownership option is *tenants in common*. This option does not transfer ownership to the other partner upon death, but you can pass this kind of ownership by a will. This kind of ownership allows you to own the home in unequal pieces. If one partner provides more of the financial resources for the purchase of the residence, he or she can own a larger "piece" of the home. You can also use this method to gradually up one partner's level of ownership in the home as he or she contributes more.

For example, if Partner A provides the down payment, both partners will share the mortgage payments and Partner B will be doing remodeling to the home, you could start out with Partner A owning a larger percentage of the home. Once remodeling work has been done and you have both put an equal amount of money or resources into the home, you can then convert to a joint tenancy with some simple paperwork done by an attorney.

The lending institution holding your note and mortgage almost always will require all parties signing the documents and listed on the deed to be jointly responsible for making the mortgage payment regardless of your ownership levels. If one party becomes unable to meet his or her share of the obligation, the other one will be held responsible. Paying your half will not prevent the bank from foreclosing on the property.

HOME SHARING

If one of you owns a home and the other partner moves in, you might wish to approach your real estate relationship in stages. In the beginning, you might work out an agreement through which the partner moving in will pay the homeowner a certain amount each month towards the cost of the mortgage and/or utilities as a kind of rent. The partner moving in will have no ownership right in the home, even if he lives there for many years and contributes toward the mortgage.

Should you reach a point where you would like to be joint owners of the home, it will be necessary to re-finance

RAINBOW TIP

If one partner has bad credit or a high debt to income ratio, you might consider making the purchase in one partner's name and then adding the second partner's name to the title at a later date (adding him or her to the mortgage later would involve a refinance). This will allow you to purchase the home if you would otherwise be denied.

However, it is important to understand that adding a partner's name to the title is a gift and can result in a *gift tax*. An alternative to this problem is to maintain sole legal ownership and then include a provision in your will passing ownership to your partner if you should die first.

your mortgage and file a deed in which the original homeowner partner transfers part of his or her ownership rights in the home, so that
you can both become joint tenants with right of survivorship.

−4−

DEALING WITH FINANCES

Finances can be a real sticking point in some relationships, while for other couples they are no big deal. This chapter will help you learn how to create joint ownership in your accounts and help you weigh the pros and cons of doing so.

CONSIDERING JOINT OWNERSHIP

As with anything in life, there are pros and cons involved in creating joint ownership in accounts with a partner. A joint account can certainly make it easier to manage household finances as a couple. A joint account eliminates complicated calculations or arrangements. You don't need to say, "You pay for dinner and I'll pay for the movie." You don't need to sit down at the end of each month and add up how much each of you must pay for rent and utilities.

Having joint accounts can also help two partners

feel as if their lives are more merged and shared. Joint accounts imply a certain amount of trust and commitment, since each partner is legally entitled to withdraw the entire balance from the account without the other's permission.

However, joint accounts can raise some issues that may not be so easily dealt with. One problem is how to straighten it all out if you dissolve your partnership or break up. Trying to go back through possibly years of bank statements to create a detailed account of who deposited what, and who took out what, is a tedious process rife with frustration.

Another issue that arises is tax law. A married heterosexual couple is basically free to transfer money back and forth with no adverse tax consequence. However gay couples are not considered legally married by the IRS and some transfers can be technically considered gifts, falling under gift tax provisions.

RAINBOW TIP

Visit the Gay Financial Network at :
www.gfn.com.

For example, if two partners set up a joint account and Partner A deposits $20,000 and Partner B withdraws $12,000, technically Partner A has made a gift to Partner B.

You may transfer up to $11,000 (as of the date this book went to press) to a person each calendar year without activating gift tax, but once you exceed that, you have gift tax issues to cope with. While this may have a limited effect today, it can have a significant impact on future estate planning and dispositions of your property at death. (See Chapter 10 for more detail on estate planning.)

JOINT BANK ACCOUNTS

You and a partner can open a joint bank account with right of survivorship (meaning if one dies, the other gets all the money without dealing with probate). Joint accounts are great for the convenience factor. When you have a joint account, you and partner can both withdraw all of the money at any time, so there has to be an element of trust.

You can choose to place all of your money in joint accounts, or you can choose to have joint accounts and keep individual accounts as well. Some couples create a joint account which they use exclusively for joint expenses and then pay personal expenses with personal accounts. Others deposit all their funds in joint accounts and pay everything out of them.

Another option to consider is a *Totten trust*. This is a bank account in one name, which is set so that when that person dies, the account is transferred directly to his or her partner (or anyone else selected). Totten trusts have long been used with bank accounts. Their use has recently been expanding to include securities such as stocks, bonds, and mutual funds.

A Totten trust is created when property is set up in trust for a named beneficiary such as your partner. Your financial institution may use the letters POD (pay on death or payable on death) or TOD (transfer on death) on the account. Regardless of the designation, you control the property during your lifetime, and upon your death, it immediately goes to your partner (*beneficiary*) without a will or probate proceeding. (See Chapter 10 on estate planning.)

JOINT INVESTMENTS

You and a partner can open joint investment accounts with the right of survivorship. Again you will need to decide if you want everything to be joint or if you want to keep some things separate. Another option is to set up your account under the *Uniform Transfers on Death Securities Registration Act*, which acts like a Totten trust for securities. It is best to discuss this with your financial advisor since there are some tax advantages available.

JOINT CREDIT CARDS AND DEBTS

Opening joint credit cards may make you feel more united as a couple, but most of the time it is not a good idea. You are much better off maintaining separate credit cards. The most important reason for this is if you get into financial difficulties, only one of you is on the line with the credit card company. If both of you are co-signors on the account (meaning you applied for it as a joint account and both signed the application), the company could (and certainly will try to) collect against both of you should the account become delinquent. By maintaining separate accounts you could spot financial troubles on the horizon and make some financial changes leaving one partner with much less to lose. The same holds true for joint debts, such as personal loans.

If one of you has bad credit, it is tempting to place all debts in the other partner's name. You need to be careful when doing this though. The only way to fix bad credit is to first pay off what you owe and then prove you handle new debt. A partner with a bad credit record needs to first get up to date and then continue to use at least some credit so that he or she can start to re-build a good credit report.

RAINBOW TIP

If you'd like to share a credit card account, consider taking one of your single accounts and asking for a second card for your partner to use. This way you can share the account, but the second partner's liability is limited.

Additionally you do not want the partner with good credit to become bogged down by handling both partners' debts. By the same token, make sure you do not put all of your assets in just one partner's name. You want both partners to be able to show a history or having bank accounts and other items of value.

One financial advantage of being gay is that your credit report and your partner's will not be linked. Married heterosexual couples' credit reports are often linked and each other's debts appear on each other's reports.

Utility companies usually list the account in one person's name. If you want to the account to be joint, tell them, but again realize that this mean both of you will be liable for the bill. Another alternative is to have your partner listed as an authorized person who can contact them regarding billing, outages, or other problems.

RETIREMENT

Gay partners are not entitled to receive Social Security benefits on behalf of their partners as married couples are. Some pension and retirement accounts permit employees to designate gay partners as beneficiaries. For example, with 401(k) plans, you can name your beneficiary. However, the tax consequences are different for gay couples than for married couples in some instances, adding further discrimination to the mix.

It is important to check the requirements of your specific plan and determine what forms you need to complete to name your partner as beneficiary. Generally, your partner must be considered a *joint annuitant* under the plan to receive payments. Most retirement plans do not allow gay partners to receive benefits, often referred to as the *gay penalty*, since hetero spouses can receive payments.

SAFETY DEPOSIT BOXES

Many people like to hold a safety deposit box at a bank to store important papers, such as stock and bond certificates, cash, and other valuables. You and your partner can take out a box jointly, but be aware this means that either of you can have access to the box and its contents at any time. You might also wish to consider purchasing a small fireproof safe (the small ones are very light and are about the size of a shoebox) to keep at home to store important documents.

LIFE INSURANCE

For a discussion of life insurance, see Chapter 6. Life insurance can be a useful estate planning tool, so be sure to discuss it as an option with your financial advisor.

TAXES

If you are part of a domestic partnership (see Chapter 7), you are not able to file your taxes jointly (except in Vermont, where state taxes can be filed jointly, but federal taxes must be filed separately). You and your partner will each have to file separately.

There are some ways to use this to your advantage. One approach is to have Partner A file itemized deductions and have

Partner B file standardized deductions. To do this, Partner A may need to write all the checks and make all the payments that can be deducted in an itemized return.

Other strategies for minimizing your taxable income include one partner hiring the other, both partners starting their own businesses (even if they are only part-time), one partner lending money to the other's business and so on.

You should also consider what you can do to minimize your taxes through *income shifting*. If possible, the partner in the lower tax bracket should take on more income, while the partner in the higher tax bracket should take more of the couple's deductions. Also, take a look at how you report charitable donations. The partner in the higher tax bracket should ideally report most of a couple's donations.

The more complicated you make the transactions, the greater the need to discuss these and other ideas with your tax advisor or accountant. However, there are any number of perfectly legal arrangements that can be made to limit your tax liability. Documentation is the key where the IRS is concerned.

It is possible for a couple to file one tax return, but only if one partner is claiming the other as a dependent. To do so, the dependent partner must be unmarried and have a taxable income under $2900 (this amount can fluctuate from year to year). He or she must receive most of his or her support from the income earning partner.

If you have children, the legal parent of each child may claim him or her as dependent. If you are both legal parents of a child together, such as by adoption (discussed in Chapter 11), the parent with the highest income is the one who should probably take the exemption. Both of you cannot claim the child as a dependent in the same year. However, you can change who will claim the dependent each year if you wish, based on your income levels and tax benefits.

You are not allowed to split the exemption (each claiming only half for a single child), but you are allowed to divide multiple children, each taking one or more on either return. In any given year, only one of you may claim a particular dependent. Discuss with your tax advisor or accountant what makes the most sense in your case.

If one partner receives health insurance through the other partner's health insurance program, this may be considered taxable income to the partner receiving the benefit. In California, the law states that it is not income, but federal tax law and tax laws in other states differ.

POWERS OF ATTORNEY

An important tool that couples should have is *powers of attorney*. It allows your partner to conduct business for you with your bank, utility company, broker, insurance company, mortgage lender, or any other individual or organization with whom you conduct business. The power of attorney can give your partner broad, comprehensive power to handle any business, legal or financial matter, or it can be quite limited, providing authority only over specific matters or situations. Discuss these options with your attorney.

Some states will still classify a power of attorney as either *springing* or *durable*. A springing power of attorney takes effect only upon the happening of a certain event—such as illness or incompetency. A durable power of attorney is in effect from the time it is signed. In some states, the power of attorney will just be called a durable power of attorney, but you can make it take effect at a future time or event like a springing power of attorney.

If you and your partner want to give each other the ability to handle each other's finances and make decisions for each other, a durable power of attorney makes sense, as long as you truly trust one another. A springing power of attorney is a good idea if you do not want to give each other that authority now, but would like to be able to manage things for each other in the case of illness.

> ## RAINBOW TIP
>
> Certain joint accounts act in a similar manner to powers of attorney. However, joint accounts are limited as to what types of property they can cover. They can also have legal and tax problems that powers of attorney do not have.

The law allows others to rely on your power of attorney, so you will be bound by what your partner does. This means that you need to have a great deal of trust in the person you select as your agent. You are giving a tremendous amount of power to your partner, and these agreements should not be entered into lightly. Plus, you must ask yourself whether your partner can make the types of decisions you need. Not everybody has the same financial savvy as others and that can include your partner. Financial decisions are a source of stress in every relationship, so make sure you both are comfortable before entering into this arrangement. You can limit your power of attorney to make it fit your needs. It is important to discuss these issues together and create a plan that works for you both.

Most states have created an approved durable power of attorney form in their statutes. These statutory forms have some standard language, and a list of the various types of powers you may give to your agent. If you live in one of the states with a statutory financial power of attorney form, use the specific form for your state. (Check with your state's attorney general's website or go to **www.findlaw.com** and click on "states," then "your state," and then on the "forms" section.)

Some financial institutions prefer and may even require that you use their form. Generally that form will only be good at that financial institution, so you will still need a general power of attorney everyplace else. Check with your bank or broker to see if they require a specific form.

A power of attorney avoids having to go through a *guardianship proceeding* in the event you become incapacitated. Having both a power of attorney for your finances and a *health care power of attorney* can allow your partner to take care of your affairs immediately in the event something should happen to you. Without these documents, a lengthy and expensive court proceeding would have to take place to name a *guardian*. If contested by your family, it is unlikely that your partner would be named the guardian, and could be excluded from making any of the decisions. This is especially problematic if you have intermingled belongs, which is very likely in a long-term relationship.

Changes to Powers of Attorney

Once granted, you have the power to take back or change your power of attorney. There are specific ways to go about revoking a power of attorney.

Some provide a termination date in them. In other words, the power of attorney states it is only effective until some specific date. Otherwise, you must sign another document revoking the power of attorney. For the revocation to be effective, you must give a copy of the revocation to the person you named as your agent in the power of attorney if he or she knew about it, or to any financial institution or company that was acting in accordance with the power of attorney. You can also choose to destroy the document if it has not been filed or given to anyone.

Power of attorney forms are slightly different in each state, so you are best served by contacting an attorney or purchasing the forms at a legal stationery store in your area. You can also obtain a form from a paralegal service. Powers of attorney forms are usually fill-in-the-blank forms and can be completed without assistance. Most must be notarized, which you can do at your bank.

A healthcare power of attorney is a different type of document that allows your partner to discuss and make decisions about your health care with medical providers. Also called *health care directives*, health care powers of attorney are discussed more fully in Chapter 5.

LIVING TRUSTS

While a power of attorney is probably the best tool for same-sex couples, other alternatives exist, such as a *revocable living trust*. A *living trust* is a separate legal entity where you designate a *trustee*, usually yourself, to manage the property. Ownership of your property is transferred to the trust.

You then name your partner as your *successor trustee*. A successor trustee takes over control of the trust should you become incapacitated. Like a *springing power of attorney*, he or she can only act if you become incapacitated. A living trust is complicated and more expensive to create and maintain than a springing power of attorney. It must have its own tax identification number and separate tax returns must be filed.

Since the trust is revocable, it can be cancelled at any time. If your relationship ends, you can change your successor trustee. The other benefit to a living trust is that when you die, the property in the trust passes outside of *probate* to the successor trustee. (See Chapter 10 for more information about wills and trusts.)

–5–
HEALTH AND MEDICAL ISSUES

Dealing with health issues is one of the most important aspects of life in today's world. Medical costs continue to skyrocket and health insurance availability and costs reflect this. Making decisions about health care can be difficult, and if you are in a committed relationship, planning so that you each will be able to make decisions for the other is very important. If you or your partner is dealing with AIDS or HIV, your health care decisions are even more complicated.

HEALTH INSURANCE
First it's important to note that you cannot be denied health insurance because you are gay. If your employer offers health insurance, you must have access to it just as other employees do. If your employer does not offer family plans to GLBT couples, talk to your human resource contact. If enough people are interested, the employer may make family plans available to GLBT couples or switch to a carrier that has family plans for partners in place.

Coverage for Partners and Families
Your employer is not obligated to allow you to obtain a family plan to include your partner, unless you live in Vermont, have been unionized, and the insurance company is a Vermont company. However, there are many employers who do offer health insurance coverage to partners. See Chapter 6 for more information about this.

If you have children and you are their legal parent, you can obtain family coverage through your employer (although unfortunately many employers now require employees to contribute to the cost of the premiums). If your partner is the legal parent of a child and he or she is covered under your plan, his or her child should be covered as well.

Pre-Existing Conditions

You can be denied insurance if you have a pre-existing condition. However, the *Health Insurance Portability and Accountability Act (HIPAA)* permits you to obtain coverage with a pre-existing condition if you previously had health insurance, but there may be waiting periods. A pre-existing condition is one for which you have received treatment within the last six months and includes HIV and AIDS. If you have a medical condition, but have not received treatment for it in the last six months, it cannot be considered a pre-existing condition. If you do have a pre-existing condition, you might have to wait up to twelve months before you become eligible for coverage for that condition.

COBRA

If you leave a job, *COBRA (Consolidated Omnibus Budget Reconciliation Act)* allows you to continue your health insurance through your previous employer for up to eighteen months. You are responsible for paying the premiums yourself, usually on a monthly basis.

Once you start a new job, you will qualify for new coverage as soon as you meet that employer's waiting period. You can continue your COBRA coverage until your new insurance coverage starts. This will ensure that pre-existing conditions will be covered. You can continue to cover a pre-existing condition through COBRA even if hired for a new job.

NOTE: *If your partner is covered under your insurance, COBRA does not apply to him or her and his or her insurance is not required to be offered. Some employers do offer this as an option, however.*

FMLA Leaves

If you are caring for a partner who has AIDS or HIV (or another illness or condition), you do not qualify for the federal *Family and Medical Leave Act (FMLA)*, which allows people to take up to ten weeks of unpaid leave to care for an ill relative or to deal with one's *own* illness. You are, however, entitled to FMLA time for your own illness.

If you have been employed by the company for over one year and have worked over 1250 hours in that year, you may take up to ten weeks of unpaid leave per calendar year. Your position, or an equivalent position, must be waiting for you when you return. You may be required to pay the premiums on your health insurance while you are gone. You can take the leave in one chunk, in small pieces, or you can use it to reduce your work time to part time.

If you are the one who is ill, check into getting state or employer sponsored disability as another way to take time off for illness.

If you are caring for a partner, you may qualify for a leave under your *state* family and medical leave act. Check with your state labor department for information on qualifying or with your employers' human resource department. Even if your state does not provide for a leave, your employer may, so it is always a good idea to ask.

LONG-TERM CARE INSURANCE

Long-term care insurance is a type of insurance that will pay some (but usually not all) of a person's nursing home expenses. Long-term care insurance can be a tremendous relief if you find yourself in a position where you need to pay for nursing home care. It can also be a tremendous gamble, since you never know if you will receive a benefit that is worth more than the premiums you paid.

Long-term care insurance is an important issue for the GLBT community. Many

RAINBOW TIP

For a list of gay-friendly senior housing, visit:
www.hrc.org/familynet
/documents/3c62b.pdf

gays find themselves in a situation where they need ongoing care, but have no children to care for them. Many in this situation look to the GLBT community for support, but find a that there is an *age-phobia* in some parts of the community.

MEDICAID

Another important issue for aging members of the GLBT community is *Medicaid*. Medicaid is a federally funded, but state run program, that pays for medical care for those who cannot afford it. To qualify for Medicaid you must meet certain financial requirements and prove that you have little assets.

Medicaid has created a *gay penalty* of its own. To qualify for Medicaid, you must *spend down*—use up your assets before you can qualify. When a married person spends down to qualify, he or she does not have to sell his or her residence if his or her spouse lives in it (however a lien will be placed against a certain portion of the home). When a gay person spends down for Medicaid, even if he or she has a partner that jointly owns the home, the home must be sold or liquidated and that money spent down in order for the gay patient to qualify for Medicaid. This is why long-term care insurance is so very important for gay partners. Long term care insurance may prevent having to sell the home, because the long term care insurance will pay for a portion of the nursing home expenses.

HIV and AIDS

If you or your partner (or someone else you love) is dealing with HIV or AIDS, you are in a difficult position. While detailed information about AIDS and HIV is outside the scope of this book, you can consult the list of resources in Appendix E for detailed information.

Paying for medical care is an important issue for those dealing with HIV or AIDS. It's important to understand that most health insurance has lifetime caps, so you or your loved one may be in a position where you run out of funding for health care. You may qualify for Medicaid, a federal program administered by individual states. To qualify for Medicaid you must meet certain income and asset guidelines. Contact your local Social Security Department office for application and qualification information.

The United States Supreme Court in *Bragdon v. Abbott*, 524 US 624 (1998) ruled that HIV positive individuals can be protected under the Americans with Disabilities Act (ADA). (United States Code, Title 42, Section 12182(a).) This means that you cannot be discriminated against because you have HIV or AIDS.

There is also assistance available with HIV/AIDS medication costs through many different sources. Visit **www.thebody.com** for a list.

VIATICAL SETTLEMENTS

Viatical settlements are another way to finance health care. A person can *sell* his or her life insurance policy to a company which will collect the death benefit when the insured dies. The insured receives the benefit of getting the cash while still alive (although there are restrictions on when and how you can cash-in such a policy).

EMERGENCY CONTACT CARDS

If you are in a committed relationship, you probably want your partner to be one

RAINBOW TIP

Health care is a very personal issue. It is your right to find health care providers who treat you and your family with respect and understanding. Contact some of the following organizations for assistance finding GLBT friendly health care providers:

• Association of Gay and Lesbian Psychiatrists Referral Service
215-222-2800
www.aglp.org
• Gay and Lesbian Medical Association Physician Referral Program
415-255-4547
www.glma.org
• Lesbian Community Cancer Project
773-561-4662
www.lccp.org
• Mary-Helen Mautner Project for Lesbians with Cancer
202-332-5536
www.mautnerproject.org
• National Association on HIV over 50
816-421-5263
www.hivoverfifty.org

of the first people notified if you are ill or injured. Create a small card to keep in your wallet or purse with the heading *Emergency Contact* at the top. Include his or her name, address, and contact information. Add any other family members or close friends you want to list as alternate contacts. You may also have been asked to complete a form at work or school as well as at health care providers' offices listing emergency contacts. Be sure to include your partner's information there as well.

Listing each other as emergency contacts ensures that you will be contacted in emergencies, but will not give you rights to make medical decisions for each other, or even admittance into a hospital room.

HEALTH CARE DIRECTIVES, LIVING WILLS, AND HEALTH CARE POWERS OF ATTORNEY

Many gay couples have faced situations where one of them becomes ill and is unable to make medical decisions. His or her family members then take over and make all the medical decisions, effectively shutting out his or her life partner. This can be a very difficult situation, but it can be avoided. You and your partner have the option of creating *health care directives*, which can dictate your decisions about medical issues in advance. You can name each other as the person you appoint to make medical decisions should you become unable to do so. You can also use these documents to name a friend or relative if you wish.

Asking your partner to make medical decisions for you can put quite a heavy burden on him or her. It is a good idea to talk to each other about what your wishes are and the types of treatment you find acceptable. It can be hard to think about difficult decisions when you are both healthy, but talking about these choices in

RAINBOW TIP

Hospitals provide state approved advance directive forms at admission. You can also obtain forms for your state online here:

http://public.findlaw.com
/healthcare/forms.html

advance will help both of you be more comfortable making decisions should the time ever come.

When you name your partner in a health care directive, it's important that you talk in advance about your wishes. Some state forms require you to specify your wishes, while others do not. You want to give your partner as much information as possible. Additionally, in some states, the form is only valid if in fact you have discussed your wishes with your partner and made it clear how he or she should make a decision. Be as specific as possible when discussing the types of treatments you want or do not want. Think about all the possibilities as best you can and try to reach an understanding together about how these important decisions should be made.

Since different states require different documents, it is best to contact an attorney to help you prepare a document that meets the requirements of your state. Some states use a document called a *health care proxy*, which allows you to name the person you choose to make your medical decisions and also to limit the types of treatment you wish to receive.

RAINBOW TIP

Remember that each type of medical directive discussed does something different. While they may overlap, it is important to understand what each one can and cannot do and decide what is needed for your situation.

Other states call these forms *health care powers of attorney*. The forms accomplish the same thing, but vary from state to state. It is important that you execute a document that will be accepted by medical care professionals in your state.

Living Will

A *living will* is a document used in some states to specifically describe the types of medical treatment you consent to should you be unable to make a decision. Living wills are also referred to as a *declaration regarding life-prolonging procedures*, an *advanced directive*, or simply, *declaration*. They are limited to one of the following medical conditions:

+ a terminal condition;
+ a persistent vegetative state; or,
+ an end-stage condition.

These documents are often long and quite detailed in regard to describing specific kinds of treatement that are consented to or requested. The law concerning living wills varies by state and releases a health care provider from liability for honoring your wishes. Without a living will, your doctor may be reluctant to remove life support, even if that is what you would want, for fear of being sued or because of medical ethical considerations.

In addition to life support, a living will can provide instruction regarding your wishes on other medical procedures you may or may not want, whether food and water should continue, or what measures to take based on your likely recovery. Whatever your instructions may be, if you create a living will you must let people know. Since their use is limited to emergency situations or when you are unconscious, if you have not told somebody about your living will, it is too late.

No matter what kind of directive you complete, it is important to give copies of it to all of your health care providers. You don't want your partner to have to dig through papers to find it when it is needed.

Health Care Power of Attorney

You need a *health care power of attorney* if you want someone else to be able to make decisions about your health care in the event you are unable to make, or communicate, such decisions. Without a health care agent, doctors and hospitals may be reluctant to provide certain medical care if you are unable to give consent or help make decisions about various treatment options. Your partner can only act if you are unable to make such decisions for yourself

A *durable power of attorney for health care* allows you to designate your partner to make all decisions about your health care if you are unable to make these decisions yourself. This applies to all health care decisions and medical conditions. It is much broader than a living will, and while they should be used together, a health care power of attorney is generally the more important document to have.

Your partner, acting as your agent, is generally expected, or even required, to make decisions based upon what he or she believes you would decide under the circumstances. It is important for you and your partner to discuss possible situations and the types of treatments you would or would not want. If you know of a particular illness or condition, it is best to write down your desired course of treatment so your partner has written documentation of your wishes.

Revoking a Directive

To revoke a health care directive, you can either destroy all existing copies or you can sign a document which states that you revoke all previous directives. If you destroy a directive, make sure you destroy all copies of it. If you revoke it, make sure that everyone who had a copy of the directive has a copy of the revocation.

Do Not Resuscitate Orders

A *do not resuscitate order* is a physician order informing other health care providers that no resuscitation efforts are to be made in the event your heart stops beating. It is also referred to as *DNR* or a *no code* order.

Generally you will be able to discuss this with your treating physician and a notation will be made on your chart. Traditionally, DNR orders are issued when resuscitation will do nothing but delay death and prolong pain.

Most people do not enter DNR orders for themselves. Instead they are often put into place by the person who has decision making authority for the patient. Physicians can help you understand the conditions faced by you or your partner and can often help you decide whether or not a DNR order would be appropriate.

HOSPITAL VISITATION AUTHORIZATION

Since in many states hospital visitors are limited to close relatives of the patient unless the patient provides specific consent otherwise, you need to make clear, in advance, that your partner has the right to visit you should you be hospitalized. If you are conscious and awake, you are able to give verbal authorization, but if you are unconscious, your partner might be denied admittance, particularly if your family does not want him or her there. You can use form 5, on page 233 for this, but be aware that different states have different requirements. Consult an attorney to be sure you are within your state's requirements.

PARTNER NOTIFICATION LAWS

Unfortunately, sexually transmitted diseases (STDs) are a fact of life. STDs include:

- HIV/AIDS;
- Syphilis;
- Gonorrhea;
- Human Papilloma Virus (HPV or genital warts);
- Herpes (HSV-1 or HSV-2);
- Chlamydia;
- Hepatitis B;
- Pelvic Inflammatory Disease; and,
- Trichomoniasis.

RAINBOW TIP

Some employers and unions offer health insurance family plans to domestic partners. See Chapter 5 or the following website for more information:

http://www.gogay.net/insurlist.htm

If you are living with a sexually transmitted disease, you carry a great burden already. Exposing others who do not consent to your disease can have serious ramifications. Many states have laws that make it a misdemeanor or felony to infect someone else with an STD. In some states, there are criminal laws that prohibit intentionally exposing another person to HIV or AIDS without their knowledge and consent. These kinds of laws are normally only enforced when the infected perpetrator actually *intends* to infect the victim and are not normally used in cases of consensual sex.

Failing to reveal information about sexually transmitted diseases can expose you to civil liability as well. If you have unprotected sex with someone and do not inform him or her about your medical status, he or she can sue you and may be able to recover even if he or she is not infected. (Since there is a long waiting period with numerous tests for HIV, the other person could recover for the pain and suffering related to this waiting period.)

RAINBOW TIP

Medical records are private and cannot be accessed without the patient's permission or court order. Thus information about a person's HIV status, STD status, or other medical information is privileged and private.

Currently, there are no laws that require people infected with HIV/AIDS to notify their partners, but there has been discussion about implementing them. Some advocates are in favor of what is called *coercive partner notification*, forcing those who are diagnosed with HIV to provide names of past partners so that notification can occur. In some states, medical providers are not required to ask HIV positive patients to list past partners. However, if a patient does provide names of past partners voluntarily, the providers are required to notify the past partners that a person they had sexual contact with has been diagnosed with HIV. HIV/AIDS treatment programs normally encourage this kind of notification, but cannot require it.

In 1988, the Center for Disease Control (CDC) mandated state health departments to establish partner notification programs, but this is done only with the consent of the patient. The CDC advocates partner notification, but realizes there would be a drastic reduction in the number of people participating in anonymous testing if notification became required. Some areas (Delaware, New

Jersey and Washington, D.C.) can notify partners against a patient's will if a court order is obtained. In Indiana, failure to notify past partners is punishable by jail time or a fine.

Of course this notification is based on the presumption that the patient provided names of partners in the first place. Many state health departments use a system by which names of partners voluntarily provided by patients are given to the state health department without linking them to a patient. The partners then receive a generic letter telling them that someone they had sexual contact with (no name given) has been diagnosed with HIV and advises them to be tested.

It should also be noted that despite a flurry of lawsuits in the 1990s, there has never been a proven case of HIV transmission from a health care worker to a patient. There is no requirement that a healthcare worker disclose his or her HIV status to a patient as long as he or she uses universal precautions (such as gloves, masks, etc). A federal court in Oregon recently held that a health care worker cannot be discriminated against based on HIV status. (*John Doe v. An Oregon Resort.*)

If you have an STD, talk to your health care provider about the best ways to prevent spread of the disease. If you have an STD, it makes sense to warn all sexual partners before you have sexual contact, since it could protect the other person's health and protect you from legal liability.

END OF LIFE ISSUES

Unfortunately, we are still losing members of the GLBT community to AIDS. Partners, lovers, and friends are lost to other medical problems as well. If someone you love is seriously ill or has recently passed away, you are in a position where you need a lot of support.

RAINBOW TIP

Sadly, there are now more than 44,000 panels in the AIDS Memorial Quilt Project. To learn more, call 404-688-5500 or visit:

www.aidsquilt.org

In facing the end of life, it is important to make sure there is a will (see Chapter 10), as well as health care directives in place. Should you or your loved one face the end of life, get help from a local hospice organization. For local hospice care information, contact:

The National Hospice and Palliative Care Organization
1700 Diagonal Road, Suite 625
Alexandria, VA 22314
703-837-1500
www.nhpco.org

Physician assisted suicide is illegal in most states, though the movement to legalize it continues to remain viable. If this is something you are interested in, visit the Euthanasia World Directory at **www.finalexit.org.**

Organ Donor Agreement

Should you wish to donate any of your organs or leave your body to researchers, you need to complete an organ donor agreement. In many states, you can sign the release on the back of your driver's license or fill out an organ donation card. If you do not do so, your next of kin will be permitted to make the choice, not your partner (unless you are in Vermont). You may use form 7, page 236, appointing your partner as the person who will make this decision, but be aware that it may not be accepted in all states. If you do complete an organ donor agreement, it is important to discuss it with your partner and next of kin. Visit **www.organdonor.gov** for more information about organ donation.

Unfortunately, many gay donors' organs are disposed of and not used, simply because the donors are gay. There is fear that a donor could be HIV positive and not know it. Since HIV testing is a lengthy process, United National Organ Sharing (UNOS, the agency the coordinates organ donation in the United States) will not accept them. Also, many medical centers will not place donated organs into HIV positive patients.

Some people choose to donate their entire bodies to research. To do so, contact a medical school in your vicinity and ask them for information about the program. They will provide you with forms and releases to ensure that your wishes are carried out.

Autopsy, Burial, and Cremation

The next of kin is normally given the authority to decide if an autopsy will be performed after a person dies. You can use your health care directive to authorize your partner to make this decision for you, but this may not be valid in all states.

Next of kin also have the authority to make decisions about how to dispose of the deceased's remains. If you wish to give your partner authority to make this decision, include a provision in your will authorizing him or her to do so and make sure you talk about this with him or her in advance. If you include this in your will, but tell no one, by the time your will is read, it will be too late. You can also write these instructions as a separate document. In most states, these instructions are upheld by courts. Specify in your instructions that you would like your partner to be the one handling the arrangements. You want to be sure your partner is not excluded by family members.

RAINBOW TIP

There is a *Federal Funeral Rule* that governs the type and amount of information a funeral home must give family members seeking funeral and body disposition services. You can read it at:

www.ftc.gov/bcp/rulemaking/funeral

Grief

Whether someone you loved died of AIDS or other reasons, coping with grief is a big part of your life. Look for local AIDS bereavement groups or general bereavement groups to help yourself cope. Contact your local gay pride organization or gay community organization for information about local groups. Local hospitals also often grief support groups.

–6–
BENEFITS, INSURANCE, AND LEGAL PROTECTIONS

Unfortunately at this time, GLBT partners are usually not eligible to receive the same kinds of benefits and legal protections offered to married, heterosexual couples. This chapter will help you understand how to enforce your rights and avoid pitfalls.

EMPLOYMENT PROTECTION

As previously mentioned, there is no federal protection for discrimination in the workplace based on sexual orientation or gender identity. Some states and municipalities do however provide varying levels of protection. As an employee, it is important to know what rights you have and what you can do to protect yourself and your partner.

Chapter 2 contains information for finding out whether your local community offers workplace protection. In these communities, a company violating or not meeting its requirements in regards to protecting GLBT workers or providing domestic partnership benefits can be found liable and forced to implement changes. If you are not fortunate enough to live in one of these communities, you may still have protections you otherwise did not consider. Look to your company's non-discrimination policy. If one is in place that prohibits discrimination on the basis of sexual orientation or gender issues, the company should be required to protect you from harassment and be forbidden from refusing to hire you or from firing you on account of your sexual orientation. Check with your HR department and company handbook to see what your company's non-discrimination policy is.

Also, if you work for an organization that is unionized, more and more major unions are pushing for contracts that contain terms to protect its members from harassment and discrimination based on sexual orientation, and provide benefits for domestic partners. Review your contract and see your union steward or representative for more information about what your contract contains.

Some employers and unions offer health insurance family plans to domestic partners. See Chapter 5 for more information, as well as **www.gogay.net/insurlist.htm**.

DOMESTIC PARTNER BENEFITS

If you are lucky enough to work for an organization that offers domestic partner benefits, there are some important considerations that you must make before enrolling your partner in these benefits. To understand these ramifications, it is important to review the general framework employers offering domestic partnership benefits impose.

Domestic partners will generally have to provide the employer with an affidavit specifying that they are domestic partners and outlining their relationship. The information on the affidavit may include information about the financial support they provide to each other and state that they live in a relationship equivalent to a marriage. Additionally, companies often require proof of commingled finances, common residence, and decision-making authority. Proof of a joint checking account, mortgage or lease agreements, wills or powers of attorney may have to be submitted when applying for domestic partnership benefits. If your company has a program in place, your human resource department will be able to provide you with information regarding exactly what they will need.

If you take the benefits offered, you will face important legal and tax consequences. If you signed an affidavit regarding your eligibility for benefits, and the information you provided is false, your company could require you to repay it for the costs of the benefits. It would also be grounds for terminating your employment in most circumstances.

In addition, and having a greater immediate impact, is the tax implications surrounding domestic partner benefits. The IRS does not consider domestic partners as spouses for tax purposes. As such, the value of the benefits you are receiving for your partner will be taxed as income to the employee. This additional income is referred to as *imputed income*.

Employers must report and withhold taxes on the fair market value of benefits received. This amount generally includes the amount the employer contributes for insurance to cover the domestic partner, as well as the cost of any fringe benefits extended to the domestic partner. For example, many major airlines offer free or reduced flying to its employees, and their dependents. However when the employee's domestic partners take advantage of these benefits, the employee will see additional income on his her pay stub reflecting the value of the benefit received. Depending on the costs of these benefits, the employee can see a dramatic rise in his or her taxable income, without seeing any additional dollars in pay. The additional taxes owed can be significant so it is important to consult with tax professionals or accounts to determine the true financial impact of these benefits.

For a list of employers with domestic partnership benefits visit: **www.hrc.org/worknet**, which also contains copies of sample policies. To learn more about imputed income visit the IRS's website at **www.irs.gov**.

RAINBOW TIP

Domestic partner benefits can include:

- medical, dental, and vision insurance;
- disability and life insurance;
- pension benefits;
- family and bereavement leave;
- tuition reimbursement;
- credit union membership;
- relocation and travel expenses; and,
- inclusion of partners in company events.

Other benefits could also be available, but do not expect them to exceed those granted to employees with spouses.

LIFE INSURANCE

When you name a person as the beneficiary on your life insurance policy, he or she will receive the face amount of the policy in the event of your natural or accidental death. A beneficiary must be someone who has an insurable interest in your life—in other words, it has to be someone who would suffer some financial loss if you die. Spouses, children, parents or other family members are commonly named beneficiaries.

RAINBOW TIP

As a last resort, you can take out a policy and name a parent or child as your beneficiary and then submit a change of beneficiary form a few months later naming your partner. There is rarely little attention paid to these changes.

Many life insurance companies do not believe that gay couples have insurable interests in each other's lives. If you and your partner own a home together, insurance companies may consider you to have insurable interests in each other. If one of you dies, the other will be fully responsible for the mortgage. Because of this, policies are generally limited to the amount of the mortgage. You can also obtain a policy if you and your partner are in a joint business venture together. This is one of the arguments behind forming an LLC instead of a domestic partnership. (See page 66 for more information on this.)

There are some insurance companies that are beginning to see the light about this. Check the list of companies referred to in the resource appendix or talk to an insurance broker in your area who can place you with a company interested in your business.

In the past, being diagnosed with HIV or having AIDS would prevent you from obtaining life insurance. This is not the case anymore. While premiums may be higher since life insurance rates are usually based in part on life expectancy, coverage is available. You may need to take out what is called *impaired risk life insurance*.

As the name implies, these policies are written for individuals at higher risk of an earlier than average death. It is expensive coverage, but as new and better treatments are developed and life expectancy increases, the cost of the premiums should go down.

Other types of policies may be available also, but additional drawbacks may exist not making them a good choice. For example, in some states, *guaranteed issue life insurance* is available, regardless of health status. However, these policies are very expensive, limited in coverage, and impose a three-year waiting period from issuance to death before they will pay out. Discuss with your agent what is available for your situation and shop around to see what you can afford.

If you already have a life insurance policy, but would like to take out more insurance, but are worried that

> ## RAINBOW TIP
>
> Shop around for insurance and make sure your agent knows you are in a same-sex relationship. More and more insurance companies are offering multi-policy discounts to same-sex couples.

you will be denied coverage, ask about purchasing a *guaranteed insurability rider*. This is a clause added your existing policy (for an extra fee) which allows you to purchase additional insurance without having to go through a medical exam.

When a life insurance company considers a person for insurance, the underwriting process usually requires a medical exam and the company will search the Medical Information Bureau (MIB) for information on your past medical history. This databank will show if you have been tested for HIV (but not the result), as well as any medications you are taking. You can pay to see your MIB file at **www.mib.com**.

Some insurance companies ask single men to complete lifestyle questionnaires in an attempt to determine if they are gay. It's important to understand that once an insurance company decides you are gay (and accordingly raises your premiums – sometimes to twice or three times as much as policies offered to heteros), your name is added to a database which can be accessed by most life insurance companies. If you believe you have been denied life insurance or discriminated against during the application and underwriting process, contact your state insurance department. For information about HIV and life insurance, see **www.HIVpositive.com**.

Lastly, before purchasing life insurance, be clear on why you think you need it. Life insurance can be a good part of an investment plan if you have children or want to provide for your partner. However, if you are single you might want to only consider a small burial policy.

AUTO INSURANCE

If you and your partner live together and drive each other's cars, be sure to list each other as secondary drivers on your insurance policies. If you do not and one of you has an accident while driving the other's car, the insurance company can deny the claim.

If you want to avoid having separate insurance policies (and get a multi-car discount), you need to either transfer title so that one of you owns both vehicles and is the primary insured person on the policy and the other person is listed as a secondary driver, or register the vehicles in both names so that you both own the vehicles. This will reduce your insurance costs (unless one of you has a terrible driving record—it might make more sense to insure separately so that the good driver can get a low rate). Having both partners on the policy will also make resolving any claim easier since either partner can deal with the adjustor.

Some insurance companies will not allow you to put a non-relative on your policy as a secondary driver though, so discuss fully with your agent what is available. If you do transfer ownership of your vehicle, include a section in your domestic partnership agreement about who gets which car if there should be a break up. (All the information in this section also applies to boat or motorcycle insurance.)

HOMEOWNER'S AND RENTER'S INSURANCE

If you rent a unit together, make sure you include both names on a renter's insurance policy. You want to make sure that everyone's belongings are protected. In the event of a loss, you do not want the insurance company denying part of your claim (or possibly all of it) because of a dispute over who owned the destroyed property. While you may see everything as joint, the insurance company probably will not agree.

If possible, you should get one policy to cover both of you. It is more expensive to take out two policies. Most insurance companies do not have a problem doing this.

If you own a home together, you will need to include both names on the homeowner's insurance policy. If one partner owns the home and the other partner lives there but has no ownership interest, the homeowner would be listed on the homeowner's policy and the other partner would need to obtain a renter's policy to be certain that his or her belongings are covered. If not, the homeowner's policy might refuse to cover the non-owner's belongings if there should be a claim.

If one of you owns the home and the other does not have an ownership interest, you can have the homeowner's policy endorsed to include coverage for the non-owner's belongings. Often this is less expensive than purchasing a separate renter's policy. It also helps avoid confusion and red tape if a claim is ever made.

Another insurance issue to consider is liability to third parties. Homeowner's insurance will pay the claims of people who are injured on your property, such as if someone slips and falls on your driveway. If only one partner is listed on the homeowner's policy, only that partner is covered in the case of a lawsuit like this. The person injured could sue the uninsured partner separately. Additionally, the homeowner's insurance company could seek contribution from the uninsured partner to help pay the claim.

You might wish to consider purchasing an *umbrella policy* which offers extended liability coverage for personal injury that occurs on your property. Talk to your insurance agent about the types of coverage available.

Consult with your agent and review your policy to make sure each party will be covered if a loss occurs. Additional discounts may apply as well if both auto and home are insured together.

PENSIONS AND RETIREMENT PROGRAMS

Gay couples are not entitled to receive Social Security benefits on each other's behalf like married couples are, but children (legal children only, or those that can prove they are biological children) of gay couples are entitled to receive benefits on behalf of both parents.

If you participate in a pension or retirement investment program through your employer, check with your human resources manager to determine if the specific account permits you to name your partner as beneficiary of the account. More and more employers are recognizing the need to provide this benefit.

IMMIGRATION

The Netherlands and Belgium grant same-sex couples the right to legally marry. Many European countries also have registries similar to those found in some municipalities in the United States. At present, the United States does not recognize these marriages and does not confer the rights to foreign same-sex married couples that it confers to other married individuals. These restrictions apply to non-US citizens, binationals, and United States citizens. So if you go overseas and legally marry in a country recognizing same-sex marriages, the U.S. will not recognize the marriage.

RAINBOW TIP

The Lesbian and Gay Immigration Rights Task Force has detailed information about immigration rights on its website at:

www.lgirtf.org

Proposed changes to our immigration laws are currently under debate. The *Permanent Partners Immigration Act* (PPIA) is a bill that will allow U.S. citizens and permanent residents to sponsor their same-sex partners for immigration to the U.S. The PPIA would provide same-sex partners of U.S. citizens and lawful permanent residents the same immigration rights that legal spouses of U.S. residents enjoy.

Countries presently recognizing same-sex couples for the purposes of immigration are:

◆ Australia;
◆ Belgium;
◆ Canada;
◆ Denmark;
◆ Finland;
◆ France;
◆ Germany;
◆ Iceland;
◆ Israel;
◆ The Netherlands;
◆ New Zealand;
◆ Norway;
◆ South Africa;
◆ Sweden; and,
◆ the United Kingdom.

Immigration and HIV

Gays cannot be refused entry into the U.S. or denied citizenship based on their sexual orientation. There is, however, a ban on entry for people who are HIV positive (Immigration Act of 1990), but there are exclusions to this. It is important to talk with an immigration attorney to determine your own or your partner's rights if one of you is immigrating and has HIV. Waivers are available, but not easily obtained. Carrying HIV related medication could be enough to prevent entry.

Another major concern for HIV positive individuals already legally in the United States is fear of deportation. Immigrants seeking their green card to establish permanent residency must submit to an HIV test. If positive, the *Immigration and Naturalization Service* (*INS*) uses this information to begin deportation proceedings. HIV positive people can obtain political asylum if they can prove they are being persecuted because of their HIV status.

If deported, many individuals fear persecution and/or prosecution from their home country, since many countries still view homosexuality as a sin, and make it illegal. Penalties can range from harassment, confinement, quarantine, and denial of medical care, to imprisonment, physical abuse, and torture.

If you are facing deportation and come from a country where these civil rights atrocities still occur, you can seek asylum to avoid the deportation. Unfortunately there are tremendous inconsistencies in the way asylum cases are dealt with and decided by the INS. (Problems of this magnitude are beyond the scope of this book. You should seek the counsel of an experienced immigration attorney.)

Citizenship

There are several ways to become a U.S. citizen, one of which involves being *sponsored* by a U.S. relative—a spouse, child, or parent. Same-sex partners are not considered to be relatives by the INS, so one partner cannot sponsor another. Marrying a heterosexual just for the purpose of obtaining citizenship is reason for deportment and the person you marry could face huge fines. Partners who have adopted their adult same-sex partners cannot sponsor them for citizenship. (A child must be under age 16 to be sponsored by a parent.)

The United States is not the only country that restricts entry into the country based on HIV status. Countries such as Russia, Qatar, and the United Arab Emirates have a complete ban on entry for HIV positive people. Other countries allow HIV positive people in for a restricted amount of time, or if they plan on becoming citizens. Countries like France, Britain, Costa Rica, South Africa, and Thailand have no restrictions. The U.S. State Department maintains a current list of requirements from other countries. You can view the list at:

http://travel.state.gov/HIVtestingreqs.html

DOMESTIC VIOLENCE

It is illegal to physically harm another person, regardless of their gender. Thus, laws about battery and domestic violence apply to gays as well as straights. Domestic violence is a difficult issue. Some law enforcement officers are reluctant to get involved in domestic disputes and are even more reluctant to do so when the people involved are the same sex. There is sometimes the mistaken impression that if domestic violence occurs within a gay couple, that it must be mutual, or even consensual.

Getting help in a domestic violence situation can be difficult. Some shelters do not welcome gays. Going to a shelter places the victim in the position of having to come out of the closet or lie about his or her abuser. Additionally, very few shelters are welcoming to men in general.

If you find yourself in an abusive situation, you have every right to call the police. Even if you are met with resistance, this can at least offer an opportunity to stop the violence and get away. You can also call one of the domestic violence hotlines listed in Appendix E. These numbers can tell you where the nearest shelter is located. (These are not gay organizations, but they are supposed to help any victim of domestic violence.)

Getting to safety is always the first step. Once you are

RAINBOW TIP

For a listing of GLBT domestic violence programs, visit:
www.web.apc.org/~jharnick /violence.html

For information about coping with a domestic violence situation, visit:
www.rainbowdomesticviolence .itgo.com

For immediate help, see the listings of domestic violence hotlines in Appendix E.

out of the situation, you can decide to seek a restraining order against your abuser. Again, this places you in the position of having to reveal your sexuality and you may meet with some opposition from court personnel. However, it is your right to seek protection from the court and no one can stop you.

A restraining order will direct your abuser to stay away from you. If he or she does not, you are likely to receive a better response from law enforcement than if you did not have an order. Make sure your order is on file with local law enforcement, so that if you call for help they will understand that you are under the protection of a court order.

Domestic violence laws tend to impose harsher punishment and afford victims greater protections than normal assault laws. Many domestic violence laws allow the abused party certain protections such as exclusive possession of the residence for a certain time period without the other party even being heard by the court. While these laws provide a means for victims to regain control, they can easily be abused. As more and more jurisdictions include same-sex couples under domestic violence laws, GLBT couples should be aware of this potentially dangerous tool.

It is important to understand that domestic violence is not a gay or straight issue and is instead an issue about violence, not about sexuality. There is very little local community support available outside of large cities for GLBT domestic violence victims, particularly for men. Talk to your local organizations about this lack of support and what can be done about it.

PUBLIC ASSISTANCE

If you or your partner is receiving public assistance and you live together, your relationship can impact eligibility. Benefits such as SSD (Social Security Disability) that are based on physical/mental conditions are not impacted by your living arrangements. However, benefits that are income based are affected. Income is calculated by household and a partner is presumed to contribute to the other's support. If the partner's income is not reported, there could be welfare fraud problems. However if you and your partner are legally roommates and have a roommate agreement, then the working partner is not expected to contribute to the other's support. If public assistance is a possibility for either of you, complete the Roommate Agreement (form 3, p.230).

PRIVACY

We are all familiar with the outing of gay celebrities. Making someone's private life public is a cruel invasion, however celebrities place themselves in the public eye and their privacy rights are slightly curtailed. However, the average GLBT person does have a right to privacy and revealing a person's private sexual orientation can be an invasion of privacy. The right to privacy comes from the 14th Amendment to the Constitution.

If someone does reveal your sexual orientation, you may be able to sue. Two important cases illustrate this right to privacy.

In an Ohio case, a man listed his partner as his beneficiary in the company insurance and benefit plan. The human resources department told his superiors and he was fired. The court held that he had no case in terms of discrimination, but that he could sue for invasion of privacy. (Greenwood v. Taft, Stettinus & Hollister.)

A federal court in 1997 held that when a police officer threatened to tell a teen's grandparent he was gay, the teen's right to privacy was violated. The court held that the 14th Amendment protects a person's sexual orientation from forced disclosure and allowed the teen's mother to sue for damages when the teen committed suicide after he was released. (Sterling v. Borough of Minersville, et al.)

–7–
DOMESTIC PARTNERSHIPS

Formalizing your relationship is an important and meaningful step. Vermont civil unions are discussed in the next chapter, but there are other choices for formalizing your relationship.

ADULT ADOPTION

Before domestic partnership registries gained in popularity, adult adoption was an option some couples considered. Essentially, one partner adopts the other. This allows partners to have a legal kinship relationship to each other. However, there are several problems with this option.

The first is that it can be expensive to hire an attorney to handle an adoption. Secondly, in order to be adopted in some states, a person's legal parents must consent to legally terminating their parental rights. This can be a huge emotional hurdle, not to mention a legal one.

Adoption creates a *legal* status between the partners, for such purposes of inheritance or to obtain victim's compensation or other payments. However, it also destroys that same *legal* status with the adopted person's natural parents. Therefore, unless they have a will, the adopted person can no longer automatically inherit from his or her parents and his or her parents cannot inherit from him or her. Parents are also precluded from receiving benefits such as victim's compensation for an adult child who has been adopted by a partner.

Additionally if the adopting partner already has children and dies, his or her estate would be split equally among the adopted partner and the other children. This can lead to protracted court battles and bad feelings.

The legal relationship that is created if one partner adopts the other is a parent-child relationship. This is not really what you are looking to do when you want to legalize a partnership. It can also be a problem if your state has an incest law, prohibiting sexual contact between a parent and child. More importantly, if you break up, you are stuck with this legal relationship. There is no way to *un-adopt* someone.

Florida prohibits any adoption by gays, while Alabama, Arizona, Hawaii, Michigan, Nebraska and Ohio do not permit any kind of adult adoption.

LLCS

Another option some couples have considered is forming an LLC (limited liability company) together. This is a business entity that can file a tax return, obtain health insurance, pay expenses, and own real property. While this choice does allow couples to get some of the benefits of marriage, the simple fact is that it is a business relationship, not a personal one. Forming an LLC will not give you inheritance rights, health care decision rights, parenting rights, and other aspects of legal marriage. Additionally, there is a fair amount of expense that goes into setting up and maintaining an LLC and doing so may require an attorney.

CALIFORNIA DOMESTIC PARTNERSHIPS

California has a domestic partnership registry that offers some legal rights to those using it.

Requirements

To register a domestic partnership in California you must meet these requirements:

- share a residence with your partner (this does not require joint ownership or joint leasing);
- not be married or part of another current domestic partnership;

- not be related by blood in a way that would prohibit marriage in California;
- be over age 18;
- be members of the same sex; and,
- be capable of consenting to the partnership (meaning that you are mentally competent).

Filing
To file a Domestic Partnership, you and your partner must complete the Declaration of Domestic Partnership (form 12, p.244) and file it with a $10 fee with the California Secretary of State.

NOTE: *The California law was amended in 2002. If you were registered with the state before this date, you do not need to take any action. Registry with a city or municipality is not the same as registry with the state of California.*

Effect
The effect of a *California Domestic Partnership* is that you and your partner are formally registered as partners. Additionally, you become responsible for financially supporting each other, which includes basic living expenses (like rent, utilities, food, etc.) and can include medical care if one person carries the other on his or her health insurance policy. This means that if one partner fails to support the other, this right to support can be enforced in court.

However, this does not mean that one partner becomes responsible to creditors for debts of the other partner unless he or she agreed to that responsibility by doing things like co-signing a loan or opening a joint account.

The California law requires health insurance companies to make coverage for domestic partners available as an option—it does not require employers to offer this coverage however.

Other rights provided by the California law include:
- the right to sue for wrongful death or emotional distress upon the death of a partner;

◆ the right to use sick leave to care for a partner or a partner's children;
◆ the right to collect unemployment benefits if a partner quits a job to follow a partner who moves because of work;
◆ the ability to apply for disability insurance on behalf of your partner;
◆ equal standing in a conservatorship proceeding (seeking to act as a conservator for an ill or incapacitated partner);
◆ recognition of the rights of partners in hospitals with regard to visitation and decision making;
◆ inclusion of domestic partners in the state simplified will form;
◆ the right to adopt a partner's child through stepparent adoption procedures; and,
◆ the termination of bequests made in wills when a domestic partnership ends (this makes a will provision leaving items to a partner invalid once the domestic partnership has ended, similar to provisions found in hetero spouses' wills).

It is unclear whether a California registry can be enforced in another state. Test cases are needed to explore this. It is possible that Vermont might honor this registry. The Full Faith and Credit provision of the Constitution requires states to uphold and recognize laws of other states. However, the Defense of Marriage Act was enacted by the federal government in 1996, defining marriage as between a man and woman of opposite sexes, refusing to grant same-sex rights in areas of taxation and Social Security, and giving states the right to decide for themselves if they will recognize same-sex marriage laws enacted in other states.

RAINBOW TIP

In addition to violating the full faith and credit clause of the Constitution, the Defense of Marriage Act violates the Equal Protection Clause, which guarantees equal protection under the law to all Americans. However, it will likely stand until a ruling from the U.S. Supreme Court addresses these issues.

Termination

A California Domestic Partnership is terminated when:

◆ one partner gives the other (or sends by registered mail) a notice terminating the partnership;

◆ a partner dies;

◆ a partner marries in a heterosexual marriage; or,

◆ the partners stop sharing the same residence (i.e., one moves out).

To make the termination legal, one partner must file the Notice of Termination of Domestic Partnership form (form 13, p.246) with the secretary of state. There is no filing fee. The date it is received is the date of termination (except for marriage and death—in these situations, termination is at the date of the event). The person filing the notice must send a copy to the other person at his or her last known address.

If the partnership included a partner receiving benefits (such as health insurance) through the other partner, notice must be given within sixty days of the termination to the company or employer providing the benefit.

OTHER DOMESTIC PARTNERSHIP REGISTRIES

Other cities and municipalities have domestic partnership registries. The list includes the following:

◆ Albany, NY;

◆ Ann Arbor, MI;

◆ Atlanta, GA;

◆ Austin, TX;

◆ Berkeley, CA;

◆ Boulder, CO;

◆ Brookline, MA;

◆ Broward County, FL;

◆ Cambridge, MA;

◆ Chapel Hill, NC;

◆ Davis, CA;

- District of Columbia;
- East Lansing, MI;
- Hartford, CT;
- Iowa City, IA;
- Ithaca, NY;
- Laguna Beach, CA;
- Long Beach, CA;
- Los Angeles, CA;
- Madison, WI;
- Marin County, CA;
- Minneapolis, MN;
- Nantucket, MA;
- New Orleans, LA;
- New York, NY;
- Oak Park, IL;
- Oakland, CA;
- Palo Alto, CA;
- Philadelphia, PA;
- Provincetown, MA;
- Rochester, NY;
- Sacramento, CA;
- San Francisco, CA;
- Santa Barbara, CA;
- Santa Clara, CA;
- Seattle, WA;
- St. Louis, MO;
- Travis County, TX; and,
- West Hollywood, CA.

Check with your city or municipality to determine if a registry exists in your area. Unfortunately, many of these partnerships are no more than ceremonial. They offer few rights. The rights that are commonly provided are the right to obtain health insurance coverage, family bereavement leaves, rent control benefits, and visiting rights for hospitals and jails.

Hawaii

Many people incorrectly believe that same-sex marriages are permitted in Hawaii. The Hawaii case *Baehr v. Lewin* held that same-sex marriages should be allowed in Hawaii, but this became a moot point when Hawaiian voters approved a measure limiting marriage to hetero couples. So currently, there is no domestic partnership or same sex marriage opportunity in Hawaii.

Canada

Canada may soon permit gay marriages. In a recent case in Toronto, a gay couple was married in a church using the process of issuing banns (weekly announcements asking if anyone had any objections to the marriage) without a city marriage license. The couple was issued a marriage certificate by the officiant and tried to register it. The registration was denied and the couple sued. A Canadian court held that it was unconstitutional to refuse to recognize gay and lesbian marriages. However, the ruling was suspended for two years to give the Canadian Parliament time to redefine the word marriage. The final word on gay marriage in Canada is yet to come.

COMMITMENT CEREMONIES

Regardless of whether you can register your partnership or form a civil union, many couples choose to have commitment ceremonies or weddings. While commitment ceremonies convey no legal rights, they do send an important message in the fight for equality.

Many newspapers now print commitment ceremony announcements. The larger papers that do so include the New York Times, Washington Post, Chicago Tribune, Boston Globe, Cleveland Plain-Dealer, Oregonian and Columbus Dispatch. Contact your local paper about its policy. If your area newspaper will not print your announcement, consider printing it in an area GLBT publication instead.

In planning a ceremony, ask friends, check with local pride organizations or read ads in local GLBT newspapers to locate wedding service providers (such as florists, bakers, planners and so on) that welcome gay customers. (In Vermont there is a booming gay wedding industry.)

If you wish to have a religious blessing, contact your clergyperson to find out if he or she will perform the ceremony. You can ask friends for leads on clergy they know who are willing to perform ceremonies. Check the resource appendix at the end of the book for links to lists of clergy who support or participate in commitment ceremonies or weddings.

The ceremony itself can include anything you wish, from formal vows to casual announcements. Since there are no rules as to what must be included, use this as your opportunity to create a ceremony that is meaningful to you and which fulfills your needs and desires.

DOMESTIC PARTNERSHIP AGREEMENTS

While currently only Vermont and California offer a true, legally binding, full partnership, there are steps you can take to formalize your relationship and make certain aspects of it legal. Creating a written contract can be important if you plan to own property, share expenses and merge your financial lives. While most people do not want to think about relationship problems when they are entering into a committed relationship, difficulties can and do arise and having a written agreement in place makes sense.

> ## RAINBOW TIP
>
> Some couples prepare two documents—one that clearly outlines their financial partnership and property ownership agreements and another informal document that lays out how they will function on a day to day basis—i.e. who will do the laundry and who will do the dishes.

Another important reason to create a partnership agreement is that most employers who make health benefits available to partners require proof of your relationship. If your employer needs this type of document, you may consider executing two separate documents—one that meets your employer's requirements and is signed before a notary (form 2, p.229) and another for your own purposes, which can contain more personal details. (See Chapter 6 for more information on employer provided domestic partnership benefits.)

Creating a written contract can also increase your level of trust and comfort. You know your partner cannot just walk out the door someday and leave you with nothing. By signing a contract, you agree to be responsible to each other for certain things and set certain parameters that will affect any possible break up. Some couples include the signing of a contract as part of the wedding or commitment ceremony.

What to Include

The partnership or commitment agreement can include anything you like, but you must be aware that only certain portions of it will be legally enforceable, depending on the laws of your state. Here are some examples of the types of things to consider including in your agreement.

Property Ownership. There are lots of options when it comes to owning property together. To jointly own real estate, see Chapter 3. In your agreement you can state what your intentions are and how you plan to arrange ownership of other types of property. To jointly own bank accounts or investments, you generally need to open a new joint account. When opening the account you can specify that it is to be owned jointly and severally—which means either of you can remove all the money at any time. You can still maintain separate individual accounts.

For vehicles, you need to change the ownership listed on the title (contact your state motor vehicle department). For personal and household property, you can specify in your partnership contract what items are to be jointly owned (for example, you could say that all household furnishings purchased after the date of the contract will be jointly owned). You can create joint ownership in specific items of property if you wish as well. You can also list those items that will continue to be individually owned. See Chapter 4 for more information on joint ownership.

Debts. Your agreement can state that you intend to own all debts jointly or to have just some that are joint. You can agree how you will share payments on these. (See Chapter 4 for more information about sharing debts.)

Expenses. You may choose to assign certain household expenses to each of you, or you may agree to equally share all of them or pay them out of a joint account. Your agreement can state that you agree to be jointly responsible for the expenses of the household and then go on to explain how you will divide these expenses. Some partners apportion this on a 50/50 split, others assign percentages based on earnings (one partner earns $80,000 and the other earns $20,000—thus expenses are shared on an 80/20 split) or create other arrangements.

Pets. It is important to establish pet ownership so that if there is a break up, you do not have a long emotional battle over custody of your cat, dog or other pet. Joint ownership is an option, but it might be a good idea to specify who would take the animal in the event of a break up. Joint ownership means joint responsibility for expenses as well.

Household Responsibilities. While these are an important aspect of any relationship, they are not legally enforceable (you cannot take your lover to court if she does not vacuum). Despite this, it can be helpful for many couples to spell out exactly what each will be responsible for. This can eliminate confusion and later arguments.

Cooling Off Period. Some couples choose to include something in their agreement about a period of time they will take after a major fight or what appears to be a break up. This kind of agreement means you agree to take some time to get past your initial anger and try to face the problem with calmer attitudes. This kind of agreement can also be important in that it provides a sense of security – you know your lover is not going to walk out the door and never

RAINBOW TIP

If you live in a state with a sodomy law, you'll want to avoid mentioning sex or sexual relationships in the agreement. Include your personal relationship in your commitment ceremony but leave it out of your legal document.

come back if you have a big fight. Again, this is not a legally enforceable provision.

Dissolution. Although it is difficult to think about it, it makes sense to make some plans for how you would handle a break up. Agreeing to try couples therapy might be one provision to include. Agreeing to use mediation or arbitration to help resolve property and debt issues is another. You can also agree that you would each be entitled to one half of the jointly owned items and each responsible for one half of jointly incurred debts. If you are both listed on a mortgage or lease, you might want to consider in advance who would keep the home or apartment and how the other partner would be compensated for this.

Legal Enforceability

A partnership agreement that contains specific provisions about ownership, debt, and financial responsibilities may be enforceable if it is written as a contract. To be a contract there has to be complete agreement between the parties and there has to be some sort of give and take, which is called *consideration*. If you agree to pay your partner $500 per month as your share of the utilities and rent, then you receive the consideration of living there and benefiting from the apartment and the utilities.

Many partners create partnership agreements as a way to make it clear how they will arrange things in their lives. They include items they do not intend to be legally binding, but which they believe helps to formalize their relationship.

Living With an Agreement

It can be hard to live with a very detailed partnership agreement. One or the other of you will always be pulling it out to look something up and your lives will be essentially run by it. Try instead to create an agreement that you will not have to think about. Most married heteros do not spend their time thinking about their prenuptial agreements during the course of their marriages. You should not either. The purpose of an agreement is to clear up some legal problems from the beginning, so no one will have to worry about them. The purpose of an agreement should not be to govern your daily life and have you constantly worrying about violating it. It should make things easier for you, not more difficult

Create an agreement if you want one and then put it behind you. Live your lives together and keep your agreement as a legal safeguard.

Modifying Your Agreement

You can modify your agreement at any point. You can do so by:

- ◆ creating an addendum to it (an extra section that clears up some points or changes agreements made in the original agreement);
- ◆ writing a new agreement, which, if dated, would supercede the previous one;
- ◆ ripping up the old one and creating a new one; or,
- ◆ ripping up the old one and doing nothing in place of it.

To understand the effects of breaking up without any kind of written agreement, see Chapter 13.

Sample Agreements

A sample Domestic Partnership Agreement is provided in Appendix F at the back of the book on page 227. Additionally, Appendix E provides links to other samples created by other organizations.

–8–
VERMONT CIVIL UNIONS

While there are many municipalities that maintain domestic partnership registries, Vermont is the *only* state that has taken action to create legal marriage-like partnerships for same-sex couples. Some activists feel the law does not go far enough, since it still gives gay partners a legal status separate from that given married partners and fails to place gay partnerships on the same level as heterosexual partnerships. Others are pleased to see the steps taken in Vermont as the first in what many hope will be a wave of states following Vermont's lead. Regardless of your viewpoint, the Vermont law is an important new step for gay rights.

MEANING OF THE LAW
In 2000, Vermont became the first state with a Civil Unions law as part of its general statutes. (See Appendix A for the complete text of the law.) This law permits same-sex couples to legally become part of a civil union. The law gives same-sex partners who unionize their relationship certain benefits and protections similar to those given to married couples. This means that any time the words "spouse," "family," "dependent," "next of kin," or "immediate family" are used in Vermont laws, they also apply to civil union couples.

Restrictions to Vermont's Civil Union Law are:
- only same-sex couples can become part of a civil union;
- relatives (parent, sibling, grandparent, aunt/uncle) may not become part of a civil union together;
- people under age 18 may not become part of a civil union;

♦ people who are not of sound mind or who are under guardian-ship may not become part of a civil union; and,

♦ partners entering a civil union cannot currently be part of another civil union or heterosexual marriage.

CIVIL UNION BENEFITS

Because the law treats civil union couples the same as married couples, it means that unionized couples are given the same rights and responsibilities married couples. This includes:

♦ the responsibility to support each other;

♦ being governed by the Vermont laws of annulment, divorce, separation, child custody and support, and property division and maintenance;

♦ the right to hold real property in Vermont together as tenants by the entirety (this means you both own 100% of property at the same time and if one partner dies, the other has complete ownership);

♦ being treated as a spouse for the purpose of inheritance and probate laws within Vermont;

♦ state health insurance;

♦ spousal abuse protections and programs;

♦ Vermont victim's and worker's compensation rights;

♦ medical care and hospital/nursing home rules (such as those restricting decision-makers or visitors);

♦ family leave benefits under Vermont law;

♦ Vermont public assistance;

♦ state taxes;

♦ the privilege of refusing to testifying against a spouse; and,

♦ special Vermont laws for veterans and family farmers.

A very important point of the law is that a child naturally born to either partner during the civil union is considered the natural and legal child of both partners.

The law does not mean that the federal government considers partners in a Vermont civil union to be married or unionized. For example, only Vermont public employers (not including federal employers) must offer health insurance to civil union partners. Private employers have the option, but are not required to. When filing Vermont tax returns, unionized couples must select "married filing jointly" or "married filing separately", but federal returns will be made as single persons. Similarly federal laws about married couples and IRAs, pensions and so on do not apply to unionized couples. Additionally, civil unions will probably not be recognized by other states.

Remember that these benefits carry responsibilities. Formalizing a couple's relationship in a civil union is a legal act that has legal requirements attached.

PROCEDURE

To legalize a civil union the following steps must be taken.

- ◆ Apply for a civil union license in Vermont. This can be done in person or by mail (form 14, p.247). At least one party must sign it and attest that the information in it is true. The current fee is $20. If you or your partner live in Vermont, you must go to your town clerk. If you do not live in Vermont you can submit your application to any Vermont town clerk. (See the list in Appendix B.)
- ◆ Within sixty days of the application date, the civil union ceremony must be completed and the license must be certified by the person performing the service.
- ◆ The certificate must be returned to the town clerk within ten days of the certification.
- ◆ The certificate becomes legal when it is recorded by the town clerk. Six weeks after the return of the certificate, you can obtain a copy for $7 from:

    Vermont Department of Health
    Vital Records Unit
    108 Cherry Street, P.O. Box 70
    Burlington, VT 05402

CIVIL UNION CEREMONY

A civil union ceremony can be performed by:

- ◆ a Vermont judge;
- ◆ a Vermont justice of the peace;
- ◆ a clergyperson authorized or ordained in Vermont;
- ◆ a clergyperson of an adjoining state whose church, temple, etc. is situated in Vermont; or,
- ◆ a clergyperson of another state or Canadian province who has received special authorization from a Vermont judge to perform a civil union ceremony.

There are no specific requirements as to what must be part of a civil union ceremony and partners are free to create their own ceremony, as long as the judge or clergyperson is in agreement. Most will want to include the words "By the authority vested in me by the State of Vermont, I hereby join you in civil union."

RAINBOW TIP

For a list of churches/denominations that support gay ceremonies, visit: www.buddybuddy.com/toc.html

For a list of newspapers that print commitment ceremony announcements, visit: www.glaad.org

Contact information for Vermont judges can be found online at: www.vermontjudiciary.org.

DISSOLVING A CIVIL UNION

Since a civil union has the same effect as a marriage, it can only be dissolved in Vermont by annulment or divorce.

Annulments are granted in Vermont if at the time of the civil union, one of the parties was:

- ◆ underage;
- ◆ an idiot or lunatic (this is the technical language used in the statute);
- ◆ physically incapable of entering into the marriage state; or,
- ◆ persuaded to consent to the union through fraud or force.

Divorces in Vermont are granted in the following circumstances:

◆ adultery;

◆ one of the partners is imprisoned for life or for three years or more during the course of the union;

◆ intolerable severity by one of the partners (this basically means he or she treated the other badly);

◆ willful desertion (one of the partners purposefully abandons the other or has been gone for seven years or more and has not been heard from);

◆ failure by one of the partners to support the other financially;

◆ incurable insanity of one of the partners; or,

◆ the partners have lived apart for six consecutive months and resumption of marital relations is not reasonably probable.

To be granted a divorce in Vermont, one or both of the parties must have lived in the state at least six months at the time of filing and have lived there at least one year at the date of the final divorce hearing. This means that if you and your partner come from another state to be unionized in Vermont, you can only get a divorce if one of you becomes a Vermont resident for at least six months before filing. This makes it very difficult to dissolve a civil union.

> **RAINBOW TIP**
>
> You can contact the Vermont Bar Association for a referral to an experienced civil union law attorney at: 800-639-7036 or www.vtbar.org.

Divorces and annulments are handled in Family Court in Vermont. To obtain a divorce or annulment in Vermont, speak to a Vermont family attorney.

EFFECT OF CIVIL UNION IN OTHER STATES

It remains to be seen how other states will deal with Vermont civil unions. Other states are probably not required to recognize Vermont civil unions since the unions violate the laws of those states. This cannot be known for certain though until there are test cases. You can probably assume at this point that other states will probably not recognize Vermont civil unions and partners will not be allowed to use courts in other states to dissolve civil unions.

Cases have been filed seeking to enforce Vermont civil unions in other states. The trial courts in those states have thus far refused to do so. In Connecticut, the plaintiff died before an appeals court could decide the case. In Georgia, the appeals court refused to enforce the civil union. An appeals case is currently pending in Indiana. Additionally, a Texas judge initially granted a divorce to a couple unionized in Vermont, but then withdrew his ruling. The partner seeking the divorce withdrew his petition and the case was dismissed. So, to date, this issue has not been resolved.

There has been discussion in Vermont about limiting civil unions to only Vermont residents, but this is unlikely to be put into place because the civil union *industry* brings a lot of tourist dollars to Vermont.

—9—
NAME AND GENDER CHANGES

Since GLBT couples cannot yet legally marry, some choose to disclose to the world their committed relationship by taking on a new name. This decision is a personal choice, and while it does not change the couple's rights, it does require society to recognize the relationship and level of commitment. Name changes also arise in TG situations. This chapter will discuss some ways to accomplish a name change.

CHOOSING A NAME

You can choose to adopt your partner's name, have him/her adopt yours, or both adopt a new last name. Some partners choose a hyphenated or combination name, such as Taylor-Barnes or Barlor (a combination of Barnes and Taylor), while other choose a completely new last name. Changing your name(s) can give a real sense of unity and cohesion to your union and may also be important to you if you have children or plan to have a family.

RAINBOW TIP

If you and your partner already have children, you can change their last names by using the same process described in this section. If you have children, but only one of you is a legal parent and the child has another legal parent, a parent with sole custody may be able to make a name change decision on his or her own. If the parents have joint legal custody (see Chapter 14), then both parents would need to agree to the name change.

TG individuals usually change only their first names to reflect the gender change. Some prefer to choose a name similar to their birth name, going from Samuel to Samantha or Joseph to Joanne, while other individuals select completely new names. The choice is yours. You can choose to change your middle name and last name at the same time if you wish.

RAINBOW TIP

Information about name change procedures are available on most state web pages. To find the home page for your state, fill in your state's abbreviation in the blank in this web address:

www.state._____.us

Do a search for name change or look for the courts section.

You can also check the home page for your state attorney general.

LEGAL NAME CHANGE

Except in states where name change is a part of the civil union law (i.e. Vermont), you will need to institute a court case to change your name. In many states, you can do this on your own, without an attorney. Some states provide do-it-yourself name change packets.

The process isn't very complicated and is not hugely expensive, although it is important that you follow the procedure set up by your state. You will need to file the papers required by your state. This usually includes:

- ◆ legal proof of your current name—usually a birth certificate and driver's license are sufficient (If you are a woman who changed her name during marriage, you need to show your marriage license as well. Most divorce decrees authorize the former spouses to resume using their previous names without further court procedures, so you already have authorization to go back to your previous name.);
- ◆ a statement that you are not changing your name to defraud anyone (for example to get out of a debt);
- ◆ some kind of reason for the name change (creating a domestic partnership is a good reason, as is the transgender process);

- proof of notification or publication of the name change (A classified ad may be sufficient, but find out what constitutes legal notice in your state, the number of times the notice must be run, and in what newspaper the notice must be published.); and,
- fingerprinting (in some states).

While name changes are fairly routine and commonly granted, certain judges have been known to deny the requests. In addition to a judge's possible personal bias against GLBT members, courts are on the lookout for people seeking to change their names in order to defraud creditors. Even if someone is undergoing a transgender procedure, a name change can be denied if the court finds that one of the reasons for the change is fraud. *In the Matter of Robert Henry McIntyre* 715 A.2d 400 (Pa. 1998). For that reason it may be in your best interest to consult an attorney familiar with the judge hearing your case to advise of the best way (i.e. reason for the change) to accomplish your goal. Some states also require fingerprinting as part of the process, so be prepared to follow the procedures required in your state.

If you are not comfortable handling your own name change, but cannot afford an attorney, you can probably locate a paralegal service in your area that will do the name change for you, for less than an attorney would charge. You can also find these services online, such as **www.e-paralegalservice.com**.

Once your name change is legal, a new birth certificate is issued in the new name. You can no longer use the old name. After the name change is legal, you will have to do a lot of work to change everything over to the new name. Use the list below to help you.

Places to Contact with Legal Name Change Information
- banks;
- credit unions;
- landlord;
- credit card companies;

- credit reporting institutions (Equifax **www.equifax.com**, Trans Union **www.transunion.com**, and Experian **www.experian.com** are the big three credit report companies);
- state department of motor vehicles (usually you will need to show your new Social Security card as proof);
- insurance companies (life, health, auto, homeowner's, renter's and business);
- veteran's department (if you are a veteran);
- Social Security (use form SS-5, see form 15, p.248);
- employer;
- passport (use form 16, p.249);
- utilities;
- Internet/email provider;
- IRS;
- state income tax department;
- schools (if you have children or are enrolled somewhere yourself);
- alumni associations;
- churches/temples/mosques you belong to or are affiliated with;
- investment advisors and account managers;
- AAA;

RAINBOW TIP

Use email for name change notifications when possible. You can cc: or bcc: a list of people and/or organizations with the information and not have to pay for a lot of stamps.

- hobby organizations;
- employee pension plans;
- deeds/property tax;
- friends;
- family;
- veterinarian;
- medical, dental, vision, hearing, and mental health care providers for you or your children;
- dry cleaners;
- video rental store;

- voter registration;
- library;
- magazine and newspaper subscriptions;
- store bonus cards;
- any pending court cases;
- catalogs you order from; and,
- pharmacy.

NAME CHANGE BY USE

It is possible in most states to informally change your name by usage only. This means that you can adopt a new name and use it in your daily life without any approval from your state. Doing so is a simple way to change your name, but can lead to possible confusion and problems with social security and taxes.

A name change by usage is informal and does not allow you to pay taxes, take out a mortgage, apply for credit, get a driver's license, etc using the new name. You can, however, tell people it is your name and ask that they call you that.

TRANSSEXUAL NAME CHANGES

Transsexual individuals often use a first name of the opposite sex (and also sometimes a different last name) when in their alter persona. There is nothing wrong with using a different name when introducing yourself to people, registering at a hotel or other social situations. The difficulty comes when you need to pay with a credit card for something or offer ID. You will not be able to legally obtain ID or credit cards in a name that is not your legal name. Instead, pay with cash when possible. If you are transsexual and are undergoing gender change, read the rest of this chapter for information about name changes.

GENDER CHANGE

When a person goes through the transgender process (also called *sex reassignment*), he or she first must adopt a new name (name change by usage, see above) and live the life of the opposite sex. There is nothing illegal in using a name of the other gender before the gender change takes effect. Once the gender change is complete, you can legalize the name change using the process explained earlier in this section.

> **RAINBOW TIP**
>
> For further discussion on TG issues, visit:
>
> www.hrc.org/worknet/transgender

Changing the gender listed on the birth certificate can be a more difficult process. First talk with your medical and mental health caregivers. They are probably aware of the fastest way to get this change made in your state. Having such a change made probably will involve a letter from your doctor stating that you now have all the normal sexual characteristics of your new sex and requesting that the gender change be indicated on your new birth certificate. Birth certificates are usually handled by your state department of vital records. (See Appendix D for a list of these departments with contact information.) Some states will issue new birth certificates, while others will amend them, leaving the old information visible.

There have been cases in Texas and Kansas in which courts did not recognize gender changes despite being amended on birth certificates. In these cases, transgendered people sought to marry a person of the opposite sex (i.e. the sex the transgendered person used to be). Courts in both states would not recognize this type of marriage. It remains to be seen how other states will handle this issue.

OTHER TG ISSUES

Certainly transgendering involves a lot more than just a name and gender change. If you are considering or are going through the transgender process, it is important to be sure you are getting the best medical and emotional advice and support possible. Check the list of resources in Appendix E for more information. Chapter 2 includes information about transgendering at work.

Discrimination against TG individuals is one of the last frontiers. As discrimination against gays is overcome gradually, the transgender community is often left behind. There is also a generally acknowledged rift in the GLBT community between gays/lesbians and TGs.

If you are in the transgender process and are dressing as a member of the opposite sex during the pre-operative stage, it is a good idea to carry documentation from your medical and mental health providers indicating that this is part of your treatment. This could save you a lot of trouble with law enforcement.

Military
Cross-dressing or transgendering is prohibited by the armed services and is basis for dismissal. Those who have undergone transgendering or who cross-dress are prohibited from joining the armed services.

Cross-Dressing
Cross-dressing is a crime in some areas, where there are laws prohibiting people from dressing as persons of the opposite sex or impersonating someone. There have been a few cases where pre-operative transgendered individuals have been arrested, but judges generally recognize that cross-dressing is an important part of the transgender medical/emotional process.

RAINBOW TIP

To find information about more TG issues (including physical, medical and emotional information), read *Everything You Ever Wanted to Know About Sex Change But Were Afraid to Ask* at:

www.geocities.com
/biblioteca_ts1/everything.pdf

See the list of TG resources in Appendix E.

Parenting

Unfortunately, there are many court cases that have denied custody or access by TG parents to their children. If you find yourself in a position where you are litigating custody or access, it is important that you (or your attorney) bring in an expert who has studied children of TG individuals and can provide testimony that it is not harmful to children. (See Chapter 12 for further discussion on GLBT parenting.)

Gender Identity Disorder

The American Psychiatric Association classifies transgender individuals as having Gender Identity Disorder (GID). While it is insulting to have something as basic as one's gender identity classified as an illness, this does mean that in some states GID qualifies as a disability, making medical coverage available for *treatment*. Additionally, if you are classified as having a disability under the laws of your state, you are then protected from discrimination against you because of the disability.

> **RAINBOW TIP**
>
> Read HRC's Talking Points for talking to employers about the TG process at:
> www.hrc.org/worknet/transgender/tg_talkpoints.asp

Discrimination

Only two states, Minnesota and Rhode Island, specifically include gender identity in the wording of their anti-discrimination laws. Four states, Connecticut, Massachusetts, New Jersey, and New York have caselaw that provides protection.

–10–
ESTATE PLANNING

No one likes to think about his or her own death, but taking the time to do some planning now will ensure that the people and things you care about are protected once you are gone.

INTESTATE INHERITANCE

A person who dies without a will dies *intestate*. This means that his or her belongings and assets are distributed according to the laws of the state. Most states divide things between a spouse and children of the deceased. If there is no spouse or children, then the deceased's parents, siblings, or other relatives inherit the assets.

Since GLBT partners are unable to legally marry (except in Vermont where unionized couples are covered by inheritance laws), your partner will not be entitled to any part of your estate. Depending on the relationship your partner has with other members of your family, he or she could be placed in a situation of losing everything. It is also important to note that if you and your partner have children, only those children who are legally yours (or who can prove they are your biological children) will inherit from you if you die without a will.

WILLS

A *will* is a simple legal document that states how a person wishes to divide his or her belongings after death. You can leave your belongings to friends, lovers, children, family members, charities or anyone else you would like. It is important to note however, that if you have a heterosexual spouse (or a unionized partner in Vermont), even if you leave your spouse out of your will or specify that he or she will get nothing, most states have a law that gives a certain amount of the estate to the spouse no matter what.

In your will you can specifically list individual items and state who they will go to. You can also simply leave everything to one or more persons. In general it makes sense to specifically divide up the large, important items or items with sentimental value.

It is best to have your will drawn up by a lawyer in your state. Different states have different requirements to make a will valid. If you fail to follow the requirements in your state, the fact that you have written down your wishes will have no effect.

Most states require that the person making the will be of sound mind and be able to recognize and understand what is happening. Most wills must be witnessed. *Holographic* or handwritten wills are valid in most states, but it is important to understand that they can be troublesome, so it is best to have an attorney draw up a will and have it properly witnessed. If you move to a new state, it is crucial that you review the requirements for a valid will in your new state. While your handwritten will may have been valid in your old state, if it does not meet the requirements of your new state, it is essentially worthless.

RAINBOW TIP

Other than the rule about heterosexual spouses, there are no requirements about to who you can leave your estate. Think carefully about who is important to you and how you can best distribute your assets.

In your will you may also state your wishes about burial or cremation, but make sure others know about these wishes. (See Chapter 5 for more information about this.) If you have a large estate, it is important to talk to an attorney and do some estate planning to preserve your assets from taxes and probate.

You will need to name an *executor* in your will. An executor is the person who will be responsible for doing the legwork with your estate. He or she will pay all your bills, divide up your belongings, sell your home, and so on. Choose someone you trust. It is perfectly acceptable to name your partner as executor. It's a good idea to ask the person you choose if he or she would be willing to do this, since some people are uncomfortable with the responsibility. Executors are usually paid a small amount for their services.

You can change a will by adding a *codicil* (an addendum), by ripping it up, or by signing a new will that revokes the old one.

When you have a will made, it is a good idea for your partner to have one made at the same time. You should discuss with your attorney a provision that deals with simultaneous death (if you and your partner both die at approximately the same time in an accident). Your will should be coordinated so that it is clear who should be considered to have died first, so that a clear path of inheritance can be followed with some of your joint property.

GUARDIANSHIP OF CHILDREN

If you are the legal or biological parent of any minor children, it is important to name a *guardian* for them in your will. This will help a judge decide who should care for and raise your child if you should die. If you and your partner are raising children together, but only one of you is the legal parent, this can be absolutely essential. You want to make sure the child will remain with your partner after your death. In many states it is a good idea to include a brief statement in your will stating why you have selected the guardian that you have named. You can indicate that you and your partner are raising the child together as a family and it is important for the child to have that continuity of family bonds.

NOTE: *You can indicate who you want as a guardian and why, but the judge will make the final decision.*

Be aware that if your child has another legal parent that is not your partner, it is most likely that the court will award guardianship to him or her. If you do not want him or her to have custody of your child, it is very important that you detail the reasons why you don't want this to happen. You should also talk to a family attorney about making your partner a legal parent now, to avoid problems should you die while your children are still minors.

You can name a separate guardian for the assets your child will own, but most people choose the same person they selected for the child's guardian, particularly if they are naming a partner as guardian.

If you and your partner have children, it is important to talk with an estate planning attorney to develop a complete plan to protect your children both in terms of custody and in terms of financial well-being.

Guardianship of Pets

Some people want to leave their estate to their pets. Since a pet is not a living person, you cannot do this, but you can set up a trust that will provide for your pet's needs should you pass away. Speak to an estate planning attorney about this. A pet is considered a possession and you can state in your will who you are leaving your pets to.

LIVING TRUSTS

Living trusts are an estate planning tool that can allow you to transfer ownership in property before your death while allowing you to retain possession during your lifetime of the items you are transferring. Items that are transferred via living trusts do not go through probate (the court procedure through which a will is verified and enacted) and thus they avoid court fees. Drawing up a living trust may be expensive though, so it is best to talk to an estate attorney to weigh your options.

Since living trusts do not go through court, it is very difficult for them to be challenged. So if you have family members who would contest a will leaving your estate to your partner, a living trust may be something to consider. See Chapter 4 for more on living trusts when dealing with finances. See Appendix E for a reference guide to creating a living trust.

POWERS OF ATTORNEY

A *power of attorney* is a document authorizing someone else to manage your business or financial affairs should you become unable to (for example, in a coma, unconscious after a long surgery, or the like). Many attorneys recommend executing a power of attorney at the same time a will and health care directive is drawn up so that you have a complete package. Power of attorney forms differ in each state. Contact an attorney or purchase a form at a local legal stationery store.

If you own a business, you can create a power of attorney just for your business that gives your partner the right to manage things for you. Most people execute powers of attorney giving a partner the right to handle their personal financial affairs. The person you give this power to is called the *attorney in fact*. He or she can deposit or withdraw money from your bank accounts, sell your investments, pay your bills, manage your real estate (including selling it) and handle insurance matters. Some banks prefer to use their own forms, so if you present them with a form executed by your attorney, they may insist that you complete a separate form for them.

You can also use a power of attorney as a tool to give your partner rights similar to those of a spouse. A durable power of attorney is one that is effective now and in the future. By making a power of attorney effective right away, you authorize your partner to handle all of your financial affairs. You continue to have the right to access and use your accounts yourself at the same time. This is a way to give a partner access to your individual accounts for convenience.

You can also choose to make the power of attorney effective only upon the happening of a certain event—such as an illness or medical procedure. You can destroy or invalidate a power of attorney by ripping it up or signing a revocation. (See Chapter 4 for more discussion on using power of attorney for business and financial matters, and Chapter 5 for more discussion on health care powers of attorney.)

JOINT OWNERSHIP

Another estate planning tool that you and your partner may have been using without even realizing it is holding property in joint ownership with right of survivorship. Property owned this way automatically passes to your partner when you die without going through probate. As discussed in Chapter 4, the language required is specific and merely putting both your names on an account may not be enough. A review of your bank accounts, stocks, bonds, retirement accounts, mutual funds, vehicle titles and registrations, and property deeds will let you know how you are legally holding your property, and allow you to make changes if necessary.

Using joint ownership for estate planning does have some disadvantages to keep in mind. Either joint owner may be able to take control of all the property at any time; either party's creditors can take it and if you and your partner were to die in the same accident, probate would still be necessary since there would not be a surviving owner to take the property. Talk to your attorney about this last possibility. You can coordinate your wills so it will be clear how the joint property is passed.

–11–
BECOMING A PARENT

There are more options than ever before for members of the GLBT community who wish to parent children. Changes in state laws have made adoption processes more accessible and technological advancements have made biological parenting possible. Raising children is an option for GLBT singles or couples and continues to become accessible for all members of the community.

STEPPARENTING

If you or your partner has a child, either from a previous relationship or from a single parent situation, the non-related partner assumes a step-parent role when you form a committed partnership. A stepparent can assume the role and function of a parent, but has no legal authority or claim to the child. Should the legal parent die, the stepparent has no legal claim to custody. Additionally, should the relationship end, in most states, the stepparent has no legal right to access or visitation with the child.

Most states follow a rule that gives *standing* (the right to file a court case) in custody cases to biological and legal parents. Foster parents usually do not have standing to seek custody of children. Some states are beginning to relax this rule. Massachusetts, Pennsylvania, Wisconsin, New Jersey, New Mexico and Rhode Island now give standing to *psychological parents*—people who have had a parenting role in a child's life, such as a stepparent.

If you or your partner is a stepparent, there are some steps you can take to protect your family. It is important to create a written co-parenting agreement (form 6, p.234) which states that you intend to parent together, make decisions together, and raise the child as a couple. The agreement should indicate that should the legal parent die, the intention is for the other parent to have custody. The agreement should also indicate that should you ever end your relationship, you both agree that the stepparent will have access to the child to continue a relationship with him or her.

The legal parent should create a will and name the stepparent as guardian should the legal parent die. It is also important to execute a Consent to Obtain Medical Treatment (form 9, p.239) allowing the stepparent to obtain medical care for the child should the legal parent not be available. The legal parent can also indicate in the child's school file that the stepparent is authorized to pick up the child, attend parent-teacher conferences, attend school events, make decisions for the child, and so on.

Despite all of these safeguards, a stepparent will still not be guaranteed a legal relationship with the child. The nomination in a will of a guardian for a child is not binding on the court and the judge will make a decision based on what he or she believes to be in the best interest of the child, which might include giving custody of the child to the other biological parent or to relatives. A co-parenting agreement may not be considered binding by a family court if a couple splits up since stepparents have no legal standing to seek custody.

Evidence of a Parent-Child Relationship that May be Helpful in Court

- ◆ consent for stepparent to obtain medical treatment;
- ◆ will naming stepparent as guardian;
- ◆ co-parenting agreement;
- ◆ documents showing stepparent participation with child's school or extracurricular activities;
- ◆ receipts showing stepparent contributed towards expense of raising the child;
- ◆ calendars showing stepparent participation in child's life and activities;
- ◆ family photographs and videos;

- stepparent's will leaving inheritance to stepchild;
- stepparent joint ownership of family home;
- joint bank accounts used to pay child's expenses;
- forms in which stepparent has been listed as parent; and,
- any other documents that show participation by the stepparent in the child's life

Stepparent rights are quite tenuous and offer little protection. Stepchildren generally cannot:

- automatically inherit from a stepparent;
- receive Social Security benefits through a stepparent;
- receive insurance benefits through a stepparent; or,
- receive survivor benefits through a stepparent.

ADOPTION

Adoption legally creates a parent-child relationship and is an excellent way to create a family. When a parent adopts a child, he or she becomes the child's legal parent. All rights of the birth parents are eliminated. The child has the right to inherit from the parent, receive Social Security and survivor's benefits, and be supported by the parent.

The parent has the right to seek *custody* or *visitation* (also called *parental access*) with the child should there be a dissolution of the parent's partnership. Once an adoption has been finalized it cannot be undone. The only way to end a parent-child relationship after an adoption is through termination of parental rights, a process that takes place in a state family court and legally dissolves a parent's rights with respect to a child.

RAINBOW TIP

For up-to-the-minute information on your state's GLBT adoption laws, visit:
www.hrc.org/familynet
/adoption_laws.asp

Second Parent Adoption

Adoption by a stepparent is called *second parent adoption*. If one partner has a child (whether it is a biological child or a child he or she adopted), the stepparent may be able to adopt the child and become a legal parent. Stepparent adoption procedures are streamlined and often do not require the home studies and waiting periods that are part of stranger adoptions.

Requirements for second parent adoption:

- ◆ the parent that is the partner consents;
- ◆ the other parent is dead, had his or her rights terminated, abandoned the child or consented to the adoption;
- ◆ the adopting parent has no criminal history; and,
- ◆ the adopting parent agrees to become the legal and permanent parent of the child.

If the child's other parent is alive he or she must consent to the adoption, unless he or she abandoned the child, had his or her parental rights terminated or cannot be located despite reasonable attempts.

NOTE: *A child conceived through insemination has only one legal parent since the sperm donor waives all parental rights at the time of donation. When a child is conceived using insemination, no consent to the adoption is required from the donor.*

The adoption procedure involves completing a petition, affidavits, and consents. These forms vary from state to state. Contact your local family court for information about obtaining forms. Once the paperwork is submitted, criminal record checks are then completed. In some states a home study is required. A state social worker will meet with the partners at their home and speak with them and view the home. Most states also require that an older child (pre-teen or teen) give his or her consent to the adoption as well. Once all requirements have been met, the court will finalize the adoption. A new birth certificate is issued naming the stepparent as the child's legal parent.

Second parent adoptions are not automatic, especially for same-sex couples. Opposition and biases exist based on personal prejudices and beliefs of what constitutes a family unit. Many judges still insist that one *mom* and one *dad* is not only the ideal family situation, but also the only one they will recognize. This attitude is slowly changing with a growing number of states expanding the rights of second parent adoptions by same-sex partners.

States that allow second parent adoptions by same-sex parents:

- California (second parent adoptions by gays are expressly permitted by the domestic partner law);
- Connecticut;
- Illinois;
- Massachusetts;
- New Jersey;
- New York;
- Pennsylvania;
- Vermont; and,
- Washington, D.C.

States that have permitted some same-sex second parent adoptions, but have not clearly enunciated a rule:
- Alabama;
- Alaska;
- Delaware;
- Georgia;
- Hawaii;
- Indiana;
- Iowa;
- Louisiana (*Adoption of Meaux*, 417 So.2d 522 (La. Ct. App. 1982) held that a gay couple could not adopt together since they did not qualify as "single people," however gay single people have adopted in the past in the state.);
- Maryland;
- Michigan (There is a current case pending in Michigan that will decide this issue.);

- ◆ Minnesota;
- ◆ Nevada;
- ◆ New Mexico;
- ◆ Oregon;
- ◆ Rhode Island;
- ◆ Texas; and,
- ◆ Washington.

Florida has prohibited any adoption by gays or lesbians. (See *Lofton v. Kearny* and **www.lethimstay.com** for more information on this case as it is appealed.) Mississippi also expressly forbids adoption by gays and lesbians. Utah law does not prohibit adoption by gays, but prohibits adoption by a person who is unmarried and cohabiting with another person.

Single Parent Adoption

In every state except Florida, a gay single parent may adopt a child. The adoption can be done through an adoption agency or privately (by an agreement with the birth mother and the adoptive parent). The adopting parent must complete a criminal record check and a home study. A home study involves a visit to the home by a social worker or other trained professional who evaluates the home, the people in the home and the adoptive parent's abilities. In many states there is a waiting period during which the birth mother can change her mind. This can range from 12 hours to 15 days.

A birth father must give consent only if paternity has been legally established. It is possible to have a birth father's parental rights revoked if he has failed to support the child. Many states have established birth father registries, which must be searched before an adoption can become finalized. If a man believes he has fathered a child, he registers. If that child is involved in an adoption proceeding, his name comes up on a search and if he is in fact the biological father he can prevent the adoption. Currently these registries exist in Alabama, Arizona, Georgia, Illinois, Indiana, Louisiana, Minnesota, Missouri, Montana, Nebraska, New Mexico, New York, Ohio, Oklahoma, Tennessee, Texas, and Wyoming.

Once a single parent adoption is finalized, the parent is the sole legal parent of the child. It is then possible for a partner to apply for a second parent adoption. This is a way around the prohibition of joint adoptions by gays.

Joint Adoption

A joint adoption occurs when both partners seek to adopt a child at the same time as a couple. Courts in Washington D.C., New York, New Jersey, Vermont (for unionized couples), and some courts in California permit gay joint adoption. Florida and New Hampshire expressly forbid it. Other states have not clearly ruled either way.

Private Adoption

Private adoption occurs when a person or couple adopts a child directly from the biological mother/parents. Most of the time, it is a good idea to use an adoption intermediary or facilitator to handle contact with the biological mother/parents. All adoptions must be finalized by a court.

Agency Adoption

An agency adoptions occurs when you apply to an adoption agency and they place a child with you. You have little control over what child you get and often have no contact with the biological parents. You must be approved by the agency and this involves interviews, home studies, background checks and paperwork. Most agencies will not place children with members of the GLBT community, although some are neutral about this issue. Finding an agency that will accept you can take some footwork.

RAINBOW TIP

For a state-by-state search of GLBT friendly adoption agencies, go to:
www.hrc.org/familynet
/adoption-groups.asp

Foreign Adoption

In recent years, there has been a lot of publicity about the huge numbers of children available for adoption in foreign countries. A foreign adoption is more complicated and more expensive than a domestic one. There is resistance to adoption by gays in some countries, but it is possible to keep your sexual orientation to yourself and prevent it from becoming an issue.

To adopt a child from another country you must not only meet the adoption requirements of the child's country of origin, which can include a residency requirement (requiring you to live there for a few months before adopting), but also you must have the adoption cleared through the U.S. Immigration and Naturalization Service. You will need to pay lawyers in both countries.

Once one partner adopts a foreign child, the other partner can then do a second parent adoption as described earlier.

RAINBOW TIP

For a list of countries with policies against gay adoption, visit:
www.travel.state.gov/adopt.html

Transgender Adoption

In addition to all of the hurdles faced by people in the GLBT community to adopt, TG persons often face additional bias. Beyond the legal questions and issues, TG individuals seeking to adopt must be ready to provide additional education to those individuals playing a role in granting the adoption. Be ready to educate the court, social service workers, adoption agencies, and even your attorney as to what it means to be TG. To make the process easier:

- ◆ search out and contact agencies known to welcome members of the GLBT community;
- ◆ bring in experts in transgender issues, such as doctors or therapists to help educate others; and,
- ◆ find an attorney with experience in TG issues.

FOSTER CARE PARENTING

A *foster parent* is a person licensed by the state to care for children who are in the legal custody of the state. These are children who have been abandoned, abused or neglected by their biological parents. Juvenile delinquent children can also sometimes be placed in foster care. Most foster parents work through a foster care agency.

Foster parents must complete a training course and be approved for a state license. They must also undergo interviews, medical exams, criminal records checks, and home studies. Fingerprinting is also required. Foster parents are paid by the state to assist with the living expenses of the children they take in, but must be financially stable on their own without the monthly stipend the state provides. The monthly stipend varies by state, but can be between $200 and $700. A foster parent has no legal claim to custody. The state has custody of the child and can remove the child or return him or her to the biological parent at any time permitted under state law.

Foster parenting can provide an excellent opportunity for GLBT singles or couples to provide a home and emotional support for children in need. It is important to note that children placed in foster care may be dealing with issues of abuse, neglect, abandonment, or other emotional or physical problems. Because of this, it takes skill and patience to successfully parent foster children.

RAINBOW TIP

Acting as a foster parent is a good way to demonstrate to the court that you and/or your partner possess the necessary skills to be a good parent. This could assist you in convincing the court to grant a future adoption request. Contact your local social services department or department of children and families for information about foster care licensing requirements in your state.

It is also important to understand that foster parents bond with their foster children. It can be very difficult to watch a child being returned to his or her parents, if you believe them to be bad parents. The goal of foster care is to ultimately reunite the family. If you cannot face that, accept that, and help the children work towards that, foster care might not work out for you.

There is a growing trend in some areas for family-to-family foster care. This means that foster families do not just take on responsibility for foster children, but become involved with the children's parents on an ongoing and continuous basis. The idea is that taking the children away does not usually solve the problems in the home, but if parents are mentored and involved in their children's lives, they can improve their parenting skills and create a better home for their children. If you are interested in helping other parents repair their families, find out if your area has similar programs.

In Utah, unmarried couples (gay or straight) cannot become foster parents. However, in many states there is a concerted effort to place gay teens with gay foster parents or to place children of gays in gay foster homes. Ask about any programs in your area.

INSEMINATION

Insemination is a medical procedure in which sperm is inserted directly into a woman's uterus, to try to create a pregnancy. There are no states that prohibit unmarried women from using insemination and there are no restrictions based on sexuality. Insemination is a popular method for lesbians to conceive. A woman can choose to use donor sperm from a sperm bank, or donated sperm from a man who consents. It is important that the donor sign an agreement giving up all rights to any child that might result from the sperm donation and that the woman also sign an agreement waiving any claims against him. If you do not use an agreement in which the donor gives up all rights, he could later seek custody or visitation. Signing the agreement is in the donor's best interest because otherwise, the mother could seek child support from him in the future.

Sperm banks automatically have donors sign these agreements. If you do not use a sperm bank, it is important that you hire a reproductive rights attorney to draft an agreement that will be upheld under the laws of your state or use one similar to the one provided in Appendix F. (It is always best to use a form created specifically for the laws of your state when possible.)

If you choose to use a sperm bank, often you are able to select a donor based on characteristics, ethnic background, hobbies, and interests. By doing so, you can use a donation that may share similar characteristics with your partner. Some sperm banks permit the child of the insemination to access the name and contact information of the donor once the child becomes an adult. Ask about this option. Many adoptive children spend a lot of money and effort to find their biological parents and this makes the process a little easier.

If you are using a private donor, use an insemination agreement such as form 10, p.240. A child born by insemination is the legal and biological child of the woman giving birth. The donor has no legal claim to the child if he waives his rights. Some couples choose to include the donor in the child's life and this is an option you do have. Be aware however that by allowing the donor to have contact with the child or to develop a relationship that you are providing evidence that could be used against you should the donor ever try to revoke his waiver of parental rights.

NOTE: *If at some point you need to request public assistance after becoming the parent of a child created through insemination, your state's social services or welfare agency will be required to seek assistance from the insemination donor, unless his parental rights have been legally terminated.*

In some states, inseminations performed by a doctor automatically remove any rights the donor might have. Other states have insemination laws that only discuss the ramifications for married women—leaving it up in the air how the applies to unmarried women. Check with your attorney about the law in your state.

When having a child via insemination, leave the father section blank on the birth certificate. If you have a partner, she can adopt the child via the second parent adopt procedure explained earlier.

A recent case in New Jersey ruled that a lesbian couple could list both partners on the birth certificate as parents, thus removing the need for a second parent adoption.

Insemination costs approximately $500 per cycle. Most insurance plans will not cover the cost, although some plans do offer coverage if the woman has a documented fertility problem.

EGG DONATION

Egg donation occurs when a woman permits her eggs to be harvested from her ovaries in a medical procedure. The donated eggs are then used by the intended parent or parents to create a child. A donated egg can be fertilized *in vitro* (in a laboratory) and then placed in a woman's uterus. The woman giving birth to the child is the legal mother of the child and the egg donor has no legal rights to the child. Egg donation makes it possible for an infertile woman to carry a child to term. If you are using egg donation, be sure to have a reproductive rights attorney handle the consent documents for you.

SURROGACY

Surrogacy occurs when a woman agrees to carry a child (which may or may not have been created using her egg) for another person or persons. Surrogacy has become a popular choice for gay male couples and is sometimes referred to as the *gay-by boom.*

Another way that surrogacy is used is when one lesbian partner's egg is used and the other partner acts as the surrogate. Sperm is donated and inseminated. In some states, a first parentage decree can be issued—naming the partners as parents and eliminating the need for a formal adoption. If you are going to use surrogacy, retain an attorney experienced in surrogacy cases in your state because it is a delicate area of law.

> **RAINBOW TIP**
>
> For information about GLBT surrogacy, visit:
>
> www.growinggenerations.com

States that prohibit surrogacy:

◆ Arizona;

◆ Indiana;

◆ Michigan;

- Nebraska;
- New York;
- North Dakota;
- Utah; and,
- Washington D.C.

States that prohibit surrogacy in exchange for money:
- Arkansas and
- West Virginia.

States that specifically permit surrogacy if there is no monetary exchange:
- Alabama;
- Arkansas;
- California;
- Florida;
- Nevada;
- New Hampshire;
- Oregon;
- Vermont; and,
- Virginia.

Florida and New Hampshire permit surrogacy, but exclude gay couples. Other states laws are unclear or conflicting.

Surrogacy is expensive. It can easily cost $50,000, between the medical and legal expenses, and the surrogate's living expenses and other costs. In most states, it is illegal to pay the surrogate a fee that is specifically for the surrogacy services. When using a surrogate it is essential to use a reputable attorney and medical providers. It is also a good idea to have psychological testing done to ensure that the surrogate will be able to follow through with signing away her rights to the baby.

After the child is born, the surrogate consents to the adoption and surrenders her rights to the baby. (It is possible in some instances for the surrogate to surrender legal rights before the birth, but most of the time this occurs after the birth.) If either partner's sperm was used to impregnate the surrogate, he is a legal parent and does not need to adopt. The non-donating partner will need to complete a second parent adoption to become a legal parent.

EGG NUCLEAR TRANSFER

A new technology would allow a man's DNA to replace the DNA in a donor egg and then permit that transformed egg to be impregnated by his partner's sperm and implanted in a surrogate, thus creating a child that is genetically related to both partners. This technology has not been put into practice and is encountering many ethical questions. There is some evidence that children conceived in this manner may have a genetic abnormality called Turner's Syndrome. All efforts to continue research in this area have been halted in the U.S.

CHOOSING AN ADOPTION OR REPRODUCTIVE RIGHTS ATTORNEY

You will need an attorney to handle your adoption or reproductive technology consents. Because adoption and reproductive technology law are rapidly growing and changing areas of law, it is important to choose an attorney who is experienced in the type of case you are interested in. Talk to attorneys you have used for other matters (such as home purchases or wills) and ask for a referral to a specialist in this area. Talk to other GLBT friends and couples and find out if anyone you know can refer you to an attorney. You can also call your local or state bar association for the name of an attorney experienced in handling these kinds of cases.

It is important to understand that some attorneys are experienced in handling the legal matters pertaining to adoption and reproductive technology. Others also have experience in locating surrogates, donors and clinics willing to work with members of the GLBT community. Some are even experienced in acting as go-betweens for adoptive parents and biological parent or donors. Be very frank when talking to an attorney. Be clear that you are gay and make sure you explain exactly what you want to do. Find out what his or her level of experience is with GLBT cases.

–12–
GLBT PARENTING

No matter how you became parents together or what the legalities of the situation are, you and your partner are raising a child together and are parents. If you are raising a child alone, you are just as much a parent as any parent who has a partner. You deserve respect and so does your child. At some point you will find it appropriate to talk to your child about being gay, about having two parents of the same sex (or having only one parent), about how he or she came into the world, and about how some people react to it. Most GLBT couples and single parents find that their children gradually pick up pieces of this up as they grow. Understanding who you are and understanding your family situation in comparison to other families is a gradual process. Check the list of books in Appendix E for some books to help you talk to your child about being gay.

YOUR CHILD'S SEXUALITY
Some GLBT parents worry about their children growing up to be gay. Some parents do not want their children to be gay because they believe that it is a difficult life to lead because of discrimination and misunderstanding by the general public. Other parents are comfortable with the notion of their children being gay, if their children discover themselves to be gay.

Most researchers and experts believe that being gay is not a choice and has little to do with environment. You are either gay or you are not. Some people who are gay suppress it and lead heterosexual lives, but in general, being gay is not a choice. Worrying that you are going to make your child gay is a concern you should not

have. You cannot *make* someone gay. Children need loving families
and again it does not matter if the parent/parents or adults in the
family are gay, straight, bisexual or TG. What is important, is that
your child has a parent or parents who love freely, are comfortable
with their own sexuality, and give their children support, understanding, and the right to make their own choices.

ROLE MODELS

Another concern for many GLBT parents is that their children will
not have close role models from both sexes. For example, if a lesbian
or lesbian couple has a son, she/they may worry that he will not
have close contact with men and will not have a man in the home
to spend time with and thus will grow up missing an essential experience. Gay men and male couples with daughters have similar
concerns. Even when raising a child of the same sex, parents often
worry that their child will grow up lacking something since he or
she will not have a close role model of the opposite sex.

Again, the most important thing in a child's life is having a close,
loving relationship with a parent, no matter what sex the child or
parent is. Many, many children in the U.S. are raised in straight, single-
parent homes, so living in a home without a parent of one or the
other sex is not unusual at all. If you ensure your child has a loving,
understanding environment at home where he or she can ask questions and express feelings, you have gone a long way towards
protecting your child's emotional development.

Many things can be done to ensure that your child has role models of both sexes. Ask friends to be godparents, even if only on an
informal, non-religious basis. It does not matter if these godparents
are gay or not. Appointing a special godparent, honorary aunt or
uncle for your child creates a relationship and bond between your
child and that person, enabling ongoing contact with a person of
that sex.

If you do not wish to create something so formal, you can make
sure your child has the opportunity to spend time with your or your
partner's family members or friends. This gives your child a chance
to see adults of the other sex often in relaxed settings. You might

also want to choose a day care, preschool, or play group that will allow your child the type of role model contact you desire. For example, you might want to find a school with a male teacher if you feel your child needs male contact. Sports and extracurricular activities provide wonderful opportunities for children to bond with adults. Choose a team, activity or group that has leaders, coaches, instructors, or supervisors who are of the sex you want your child to have contact with.

Some gay families team up with gay families of the opposite sex to create cooperative family units so their children can have role models of both sexes. For example, a gay male couple might team up with friends who are a lesbian couple. They go on outings together, spend time at each other's homes, and make themselves emotionally available to each other's children.

It is possible to get too hung up on the role model concept. The best role models are parents regardless of their sex. You are your child's best role model. Your sex has nothing to do with teaching your child to be kind, respectful, fair, thoughtful, fun, caring, energetic, or any other quality you deem important. Your love and attention are the best role models.

DEALING WITH DISCRIMINATION

Unfortunately some people in your life and your child's life may have less of an accepting attitude about your sexuality than you would like. You never really know when discrimination will rear its ugly head. Remember that no one can change the reality of your situation. You and your partner, if you have one, are parents and no one's opinion can change that. You are a real family and if others do not understand, it is their loss.

Unfortunately, the decisions you have made regarding how you will personally deal with discrimination may not be available to your child. You will need to help your child learn how to cope with comments, looks, jokes, and insults made by other children and adults. The best way to do this is to help your child learn by example. Talk about incidents that have happened to you. Talk about how you felt, how you reacted and what happened. If incidents happen when you are with your child, talk about them afterwards. You cannot pretend to your child that these kinds of things will not happen, because it is a reality that some people simply do not respect and understand members of the GLBT community.

If you feel your child is having a very hard time coping with people's reactions, consider your options. Get to know the children your child plays with. Become a presence and let them see there is nothing weird or mysterious about you. If children in your neighborhood are causing problems, consider talking to their parents. Become an important part of your community and show your neighbors that you and your family are just like they are.

Join a GLBT family group so your child can interact with peers in similar family situations. (You can find such a group by contacting your local pride organization. See Appendix E for information.)

SAFE SCHOOLS

One of your greatest concerns as a parent is probably being sure your child is comfortable and accepted at school. Before your child enters a school, there are several ways to evaluate how GLBT friendly it is. Meet with the principal or other administrator and ask if the school provides training to teachers about GLBT families and issues. Ask if the school has non-discrimination policies in place with regard to employment. Find out if GLBT issues are included in the curriculum in any way.

RAINBOW TIP

Get more information about inclusiveness at schools and GSAs from the Gay-Lesbian Straight Education Network at 212-727-0135 or: www.glsen.org.

Check school publications, such as handbooks and applications, and look for inclusive language (generally, the use of "parents" instead of "mother" and "father"). Talk to teachers and get a sense as to how children of GLBT parents are accepted and if there are any resources available for them. In particular, find out if the school has a *Gay-Straight Alliance* (GSA), a group that supports students of

GLBT families (as well as gay teens in high schools).

If your school does not have a GSA, think about starting one. The 1984 *Equal Access Law* held that schools that receive federal funds and have a *limited open forum* (meaning they allow other non-curriculum based groups to meet and use school resources) cannot discriminate about what types of groups they permit. So, if your school gets federal money and currently has other non-curriculum groups, you cannot be denied the right to start a GSA.

> ## RAINBOW TIP
>
> Massachusetts has one of the better known Safe Schools Program for Gays and Lesbians. To read about the program, visit:
>
> www.doe.mass.edu/hssss

The best advice is to get to know teachers and administrators at your school. Should a problem develop at school, you will already have a relationship with those who can make a difference for your child. If you do not get the help or response you need, go to the board of education. If you still cannot get the issue resolved, consider filing a Title IX complaint with the Office of Civil Rights in the U.S. Department of Education. Visit **www.ed.gov/offices/OCR** for more information about U.S. Department of Education's Office of Civil Rights.

SUMMER CAMPS
Finding a GLBT friendly summer camp can be as much of a concern as finding a school. Talk to camp administrators in advance, look for inclusive language in camp publications and ask about GLBT training for camp counselors. For a list of GLBT friendly summer camps, visit **www.hrc.org/familynet/chapter.asp?article=288**.

PARENTING AFTER A BREAK UP
If you and a partner break up, one of your biggest concerns will be for your children. How the situation is handled will depend how your parenting relationship has been created.

Joint Legal Parents

If you and you partner are both legal parents of your child or children, custody will be handled just as it is for straight parents. Your state's family court has jurisdiction, or the right to decide this case.

Once you and your partner are no longer living together, it is important to determine parenting schedules. This is for your own sanity as well as to provide stability to your child. You and your partner can decide for yourselves how you will share time with your child, use mediation to help you reach an agreement or you can appear in court, have a trial and allow the judge to decide. It makes the most sense to try to make a decision yourselves, since you know your child best and know what will work best in your lives. Realize that the court must approve your decision, but that generally judges will go along with agreements created by parents as long as they seem reasonable.

You will end up with a written court order that sets out the parameters of your legal agreement. It is also a good idea to create an informal parenting plan that will help you deal with every day issues. This kind of agreement is not meant to be legally enforceable, but is meant to give you some guidelines to live by. (See the sample parenting plan in Appendix F.)

In most states, there are two kinds of custody that must be decided. *Legal custody* means decision-making power. Parents who have joint legal custody make decisions about the child together. If one parent has sole legal custody it means that he or she makes the important decisions about the child—where he or she goes to school, whether he or she will receive medical treatment and so on.

Physical or *residential custody* has to do with where the child lives. If you decide to share joint residential custody, it means that your child will share your homes equally and usually share equal amounts of time with both of you. If one parent is given residential custody, it means the child will live primarily with him or her. The other parent normally has access, also called *parenting time* or *visitation*.

In deciding how you will arrange custody and access, think about your schedules. If one parent works third shift, it does not make sense for him or her to have the child live at his or her home most of the week, since a sitter would need to be home with the child at night while the parent works.

Most importantly, take your child's needs into consideration when determining how you will share time. Toddlers just cannot handle alternating homes every other day. Teenagers need to have time to see friends, do homework, and hold a job. Children should never be used in an effort to get back at your partner.

Remain flexible and adjust your plan as your child gets older. Try to be flexible to each other's needs as well. You might need to make adjustment to the schedule this month and your former partner might need to make an adjustment next month. Try to cut each other some slack.

Most couples prefer to have *joint legal custody*. This means you and your former partner will need to find a way to work together, talk together, and make decisions, even though you are no longer life partners. It takes a lot of work and effort to build this kind of relationship, but it is very important for your child that you try to do so.

Remember that even though your relationship has ended, you will be parents together for the rest of your lives. You need to develop a new relationship based on this fact. Despite your personal feelings for each other, you need to find a way to communicate and cooperate with each other when it comes to your child.

Sample Access Schedule

Parent A: Monday-Thursday and every other weekend.

Parent B: Wednesday from after school to 8 pm, every other weekend from Friday at 3 to Sunday at 5. Parent B will have two weeks during summer vacation.

Holidays to be alternated every other year. Holidays alternated include: New Year's Day, Easter/Passover, Memorial Day, Fourth of July, Labor Day, Halloween, Thanksgiving, the day after Thanksgiving, Christmas Eve, Christmas Day or Hanukkah. The child's birthday will be alternated or shared.

One Legal Parent

If you and your partner are parenting together, but only one of you is the child's legal parent, you are in a difficult situation. According to the law, the parent who has been legally named as the parent is the only one who technically has any right to the child. (See the section on stepparenting in Chapter 11 for more information about this situation.) The other parent, who is in a stepparent position, has no legal right to custody, and rarely will be granted access or visitation with the child.

However, in most instances, except when the stepparent has been or is likely to be abusive towards the child or presents a danger to him or her, it is important to the child he or she continue to have a relationship with the stepparent. The stepparent has played an important role in the child's life. He or she has become an emotional parent for the child, even if he or she might not be a legal parent. If you are the legal parent, it is a good idea to agree to an informal arrangement which will allow the stepparent to have a continuing role in the child's life. In general it is not a good idea to agree to a formal written arrangement, because this could be used by the stepparent in the future to seek custody from you.

If you are the stepparent, unfortunately, all the cards are in the other parent's hands. He or she has the legal right to call the shots about whether or not you will see the child. Try to appeal to his or her sense of fairness and base your argument on what is best for the child. If he or she absolutely refuses to allow you to see the child, see if there are relatives or friends who could argue your point or find some way to allow you time with the child at their homes.

RAINBOW TIP

GLBT Parenting Resources:
  www.proudparenting.com
  www.lesbian.org
  www.familypride.org
  www.queerparents.org
  www.familieslikeours.org
  www.ourfamily.org
  www.gayfamilyoptions.org
  www.colage.org
  www.pflag.org

–13–
ENDING A DOMESTIC PARTNERSHIP

Ending a relationship is painful. If you and your partner were living together and/or entered into a domestic partnership, the end of a relationship means a lot of decisions—about belongings, the home, finances, and perhaps children. Remember that if you have entered into a Vermont Civil Union, you need to follow the divorce procedure in Vermont. (Read Chapter 8 for details concerning this situation.)

ENDING A RELATIONSHIP THAT HAD NO WRITTEN AGREEMENT

Most same-sex couples who share their lives and home do so without any written agreement. If you and your partner were living together, but never created a written agreement, it can be hard to divide things up if you had no clear understanding about ownership.

Personal Belongings

When dividing personal belongings, first separate out what belonged to each of you before you became partners. Next list everything that is jointly owned. (Use the Division of Property form 8, p.237 to assist you.) If you can, sit down together and try to work on the list together. You each can complete this form separately and then meet to try to negotiate the items you disagree about.

If you cannot agree, you may need to consider how a court would decide this issue. Whoever paid for the item is considered its legal owner, unless it was purchased and then given as a gift to the other partner. So if your partner purchased a new dining room set, but gave it to you for your birthday, it would be yours. If each of you contributed to the cost of an item, you would own it jointly. In that kind of situation, one partner can buy the other partner out, you can jointly sell it and split the proceeds, or you can work out an agreement where one partner gets the jointly purchased dining room set and one partner gets the jointly purchased living room furniture.

RAINBOW TIP

Remember that it is really just *stuff* and in the end, you can always get more *stuff*. People often fight over possessions as a way to resolve feelings about the relationship and to vocalize their anger and hurt. Keep this in the back of your mind and try to deal with the possessions in an unemotional way. To find a GLBT friendly therapist near you to help you get through this difficult time call THE-888-4564 or visit:

www.wrnetwork.net
/gay-friendly.htm

Tips for Dividing Things

Things to keep in mind when dividing property include:

◆ keep those items you came into the relationship with;
◆ keep those items you inherited while in the relationship; and,
◆ keep those items that were gifts to you during the relationship.

For disputed items:

◆ consider which partner has used an item the most;
◆ consider who will get the most use out of an item;
◆ try to divide duplicate items (one blender or TV to each person);
◆ consider selling items neither of you really wants or needs and splitting the proceeds;
◆ try to keep sets together (china, silverware, collections, matching furniture);
◆ try not to ask for things out of spite or for revenge;
◆ decide if you want to take a purely monetary approach (each partner to end up with roughly the same total value at the end) or an equitable approach (dividing things based on what seems fair and not necessarily in a completely even way); and,

◆ if you have children, it usually makes sense for the partner who
   will be with the children most of the time to keep the residence and a lot of the furniture and household items.

Residence

If you are renting and one partner's name is on the lease, he or she
will legally be the person entitled to remain in the residence. If you
decide that it makes more sense for the other partner to keep the
apartment, he or she will need to sign a new lease with the landlord
or sublet the apartment from the other partner. If you are joint tenants, whoever keeps the apartment should sign a new lease with the
landlord so that the partner moving out will no longer be legally
responsible for rent.

If you own a home and it
is in one partner's name, he
or she will keep the home
(unless you can prove you
had an agreement to the contrary). If you jointly own the
home, you can sell it and
both move out or one partner
can buy out the other partner's interest in the home
(make sure a new deed is
recorded reflecting this).

RAINBOW TIP

You may need to get your home
appraised so that you can determine
its actual value and make decisions
about ownership with that in mind.
For a referral to a GLBT friendly
appraiser, visit:

www.homelounge.com

NOTE: *If you are both listed on the mortgage, re-financing will be necessary if one partner is going to keep the home. You need to remove the
other partner from the mortgage and refinancing is the simplest way to
do this.*

If you have children, you will want to consider who they will
live with when deciding who will keep the home or apartment.
Children need continuity and it is important for them to be able to
remain in their own home, if at all possible. Some couples take the
approach of keeping the children in the home and then alternating

which parent will stay with them on a regular basis. Both partners would continue to own the home or share the lease in this kind of circumstance. Choose what works best for your family.

Debts

Each of you will be responsible for debts that are in your own names. If you have any joint debts, you are both responsible for them and will either need to pay them off together or work out a trade (one partner pays the Visa bill and one partner pays the electric bill – or the partner that pays the Visa bill gets to keep the jointly purchased waterbed). If one person is going to be solely responsible for a joint debt, it is a good idea to refinance that debt into his or her sole name, otherwise the other partner remains legally responsible for the debt to the creditor.

It is important to close all joint accounts when you split up. If you do not, your partner could go charge a huge item and you would be jointly responsible for it. If you are keeping an account open in order to pay it off (whether jointly or singly), ask the credit card company to cancel user privileges on the account, so that you can continue to pay it off, but neither of you can charge another dime to it.

> **RAINBOW TIP**
>
> You need to keep making joint payments on debts, loans, and mortgages once you break up until you can reach a permanent solution. Stick to the financial arrangements you had while you were together, until you can reach a permanent agreement about how you will divide things. Do not get into a situation where you have late fees and interest to cope with.

Support

In some states, most particularly California, a court could find that you and your partner had an oral agreement that created a contract for support. For example, you might have agreed that one partner would stay home and care for the children while the other would support the family. This kind of agreement has been found to exist by California courts and based on this, a court can decide that the working partner has an obligation to support the non-working partner after the break up. In other states, this kind of oral agreement is less clear and not as likely to be upheld by a court.

Children

If you and your partner have children, read Chapter 12 to find out what your options are when you break up. Remember that you have the right to seek temporary custody and temporary child support in family court if you are the legal parent of the child. You can seek this assistance as soon as you break up and the court will issue temporary orders to get your family through the break up until final decisions can be made.

The break up will have a huge impact on your children, whether you and your former partner were joint legal parents or not. When an adult in a parenting role leaves a home, it has an effect on any children in the home. Take your child's feelings seriously and be patient. If you feel your child is having a very difficult time dealing with the loss or with sadness or anger associated with the breakup, consider taking him or her to therapist that specializes in working with children. Contact your pediatrician for a referral.

Arbitration and Mediation

If you and your partner are having a difficult time resolving who gets what, consider seeing a *mediator* or *arbitrator*. A mediator acts as a neutral third part and works to help you reach a mutually agreeable solution. Mediation is a great option because it is non-confrontational and allows the two of you to decide together how you will divide things. It is also helpful because it gives you negotiating tools to use should

RAINBOW TIP

To find a mediator or arbitrator, call your local bar association for a referral or contact The Association for Conflict Resolution at 202-667-9700 or visit:

www.acresolution.org

future problems pop up that the two of you will need to deal with together.

Arbitration is more like going to court. You and your partner would both explain the problem and your positions to the arbitrator. He or she might ask you questions and get more information. The arbitrator would then make a decision for you. Arbitration can be binding (having the effect of a court-ruling) or non-binding (has no legal authority).

Collaborative Law

A growing trend in the legal field is what is known as *collaborative law*. The idea of collaborative law is that each party is represented by an attorney, but instead of going face to face, the attorneys try to work together to find a solution that will work best for the clients. Instead of each lawyer going full speed ahead to try to get the absolute most for his or her client, the approach is more moderate and is similar to mediation. More and more attorneys are becoming involved with or aware of collaborative law.

This approach can work well in a GLBT break up where there is not a clear body of cohesive law available in the court system (like there is for married couples) to help the couple manage all the aspects of their break up. To find attorneys willing to take a collaborative law approach with you and your ex, contact your local or state bar association or look for attorneys advertising in your local pride phone book or other publications.

RAINBOW TIP

Once you have made a final decision to split, try to sit down and have a business-like meeting about all of the issues you need to decide about. You might find that it helps to set ground rules for the meeting: the meeting will deal only with financial matters and personal possessions; neither of you will discuss emotional or personal matters until after the business meeting is done; and, you will both refrain from raising your voices or using insulting or abusive language. Give this method a few tries before abandoning it and seeking professional assistance.

Your Options in Court

The legal system is unfortunately not set up to deal very well with the end of a GLBT relationship. Gays cannot resolve their break up issues (other than custody and child support) in family court like other couples. If you and your partner have no written partnership agreement and cannot agree about how to divide your belongings and debts, one partner can sue the other in small claims court (each state's small claim court has a dollar limit on the amount you can sue for, so find out what that is first by checking your state's web site) or in a higher court. If you use small claims court, you usually will not need attorneys, but if you exceed the small claims dollar amount and have to go to a higher court, you will likely need attorneys.

Your Freedom to Decide

It is important to remember that the two of you can agree to divide your belongings and end your relationship in anyway you want to. Since you are not bound by divorce laws (except in Vermont), you have this freedom. If one of you needs some additional cash to get on his or her feet after the break up, you can decide to work out some kind of informal *alimony* payment. If you want to continue to jointly own the jet ski, you can. If you both agree to it, do it. Whatever works for both of you is completely ok, so feel free to be creative, but make sure that whatever you decide will really work. The only area where you may not have complete control is when it comes to children.

ENDING A RELATIONSHIP WITH A WRITTEN AGREEMENT

If you and your partner filed with a domestic partner registry, you will need to contact the registry to determine the procedure for dissolving the partnership. Usually this involves filing another piece of paper stating that the partnership has been dissolved. If you and your partner have a Partnership Agreement, Commitment Contract or other written agreement, you will probably want to abide by what it says about break ups. If the contract does not address break ups at all, then you will proceed as if you did not have a contract (see earlier in this chapter).

Be aware that your contract may or may not be legally binding. If you decide that the terms of the contract are unfair or you simply do not agree with them, you should see an attorney to determine if you are bound by it. You can also choose to see a mediator or arbitrator or collaborative lawyers to help you resolve issues you do not agree on. It is also important to note that you and your ex can choose not to abide by the terms of the written agreement. If you both agree to do something other than what is written in it, there is no one to stop you.

Support
If you have registered your partnership in California, you need to be aware that there is a possibility that the courts could interpret the registration to mean that you have agreed to support one another even after the break up. When you register in California you agree to support each other financially. This agreement could be used to determine ongoing support. For example, if one partner were to remain home with the children and the other supported them, a court could find that there is an ongoing obligation to provide support to the other partner.

Enforcing Your Agreement
If you have a Partnership Agreement, but your partner does not follow its provisions, you will need to see an attorney and seek to have it enforced in court. The laws vary from state to state on how these agreements are handled, but often they are considered to be simple contracts and are enforced according to the state's contract interpretation laws.

PALIMONY
Palimony came into being after the landmark 1976 California case *Marvin v. Marvin*, which held that when an unmarried hetero couple broke up, there was an implied contract in existence that one of the partners had agreed to support the other. The court then ordered alimony-like payments to be made. In 1988, another case extended this ruling to include gay couples in California.

The key to palimony cases is that there must be an implied contract between the two partners that one will support the other in order for palimony to be ordered after the break up. A recent California case (*Robertson v. Reinhart*) found that a lesbian couple did not have an implied contract and so no palimony was ordered.

Talk to an attorney in your state about the status of palimony law in your state. To avoid palimony issues, you should specify in your partnership agreement that no palimony will be paid after a break up or specify that during the term of your relationship neither partner will make payments to the other that can be considered support.

RAINBOW TIP

Find out more about palimony at:
www.palimony.com or
www.gaylawnet.com

COPING WITH A BREAK UP

Getting through the ending of a partnership is one of the most difficult things you will face. You will go through that awkward period for some time where you find things that belong to the other person and where you have to see each other to make final arrangements and decisions. Remember that you do not have to handle a break up alone. There are many therapists and counseling services that are GLBT-friendly (use **www.glitse.com** to find one near you) and you can rely on friends and family as well to help you through the rough patches.

Some couples choose to have a dissolution ceremony, which allows them to formally end their partnership and get some closure. Dissolution ceremonies could include a ceremonial burning of your partnership contract, formally saying some things to each other to end the partnership, blowing out a unity candle, or anything else that both of you agree to do. If your partner does not agree to one, you can have one by yourself as a way to formally end the relationship, find closure, and give yourself permission to move on.

Many couples have bitter, nasty disputes over money, belongings, and debt. It is important to take a step back and think about what you are really arguing about. Are you really that upset that your partner thinks he or she should take the French cookware set or is the anger and animosity really about the break up and your relationship problems? Fighting over belongings is a way to continue your relationship and a way to continue to hurt each other.

You may find that your hetero friends and family just do not understand or want to understand what you are going through. Some people simply do not credit GLBT relationships as being as serious and meaningful as straight relationships. Additionally you may encounter people who really believe gays never have long term partners and that breaking up should not be a big deal for you. Being misunderstood and brushed aside like this can make your pain worse.

RAINBOW TIP

For more information and support relating to GLBT break ups, visit:
www.budddybuddy.com
/hertz-1.html
www.gaytoday.badpuppy.com
www.q-notes.com/bms4.htm
www.glitse.com

It certainly does not help that the legal systems in most states do not provide clear procedures for ending a GLBT partnership as they do for marriage. Seek out friends and family who do understand. Talk to GLBT friends who have experienced break ups. Remember that what you are feeling is real and you have the right to mourn and grieve for your relationship.

Give yourself time to get over your break up. Do not expect to bounce back right away. Coping with the end of a relationship requires a grieving process. If you have children, expect the break up to be very difficult for them, even if one partner is not a legal parent. It is very possible to be an emotional parent without being a legal parent. Be sensitive to your children's needs during this time.

–14–
GLBT RIGHTS IN A TRADITIONAL MARRIAGE

Many gays or lesbians marry people of the opposite sex. Many do this before they come to understand and/or accept their own sexuality. Others marry in spite of their sexuality. Whatever the circumstances, if you and your heterosexual spouse are happy and want to remain married, nothing should stop you. There are couples who remain happily married, yet find sexual satisfaction elsewhere. If you are bisexual or TG, the same applies. You can continue to remain in your marriage and/or have sexual intimacy with your spouse while maintaining a bisexual or TG lifestyle if you and your spouse are happy with the arrangement.

If your spouse is not aware you are gay or bi-sexual and he or she does not know you are seeing people of the same-sex, you run the risk of hurting him or her should the information ever come out. When or if to share this information with your spouse is a decision only you can make.

TRANSGENDERS AND MARRIAGE

TG individuals are in a unique situation when it comes to traditional marriage. If a person is married to a person of the opposite sex and transgenders during the marriage, the marriage would still be legal in most states. This is particularly true in states where TG individuals are not permitted to change their sex on their birth certificates. For example, if Jose legally becomes a woman and then marries Sondra, this would be considered a legal marriage in many places. In the 1997 California case of Joshua Vecchione, the wife of a man who transgendered during the marriage tried to nullify the marriage and deprive the man of custody rights to their children. The court held the marriage was valid.

The other situation to consider is a person who has transgendered and then marries a person who is the opposite sex from his or her new transgender sex. In states where sex can be changed on the birth certificate, this kind of marriage would be legal. However, courts in both Texas and Kansas have held that a man who had transgendered to female and then married a male had no right to inherit from the male spouse after the spouse's death because the marriage was not legal.

DIVORCE

Often when a person discovers or reveals that he or she is gay, his or her spouse wishes to end the marriage. Keep in mind that ending your marriage does not have to mean you are ending your friendship, connection, or that you have to stop living together. It definitely does not mean that you stop being parents together (if you have children).

Many states offer *no fault divorces*. This means neither spouse has to blame the other or say that he or she did something wrong. You can simply say you have *irreconcilable differences*. In some states, no fault is not an option and you need a reason for the divorce. In these states a spouse can often claim that the other treated him or her cruelly and inhumanly without offering too many details.

> **RAINBOW TIP**
>
> For more information about mediation, contact the Association for Conflict Resolution at 202-667-9700 or visit:
>
> www.acresolution.org

If your spouse is the one filing for divorce, he or she may be quite angry and hurt and may choose to include specifics in the divorce papers as a way of striking back. If you are facing or considering a divorce, it is a good idea to talk to an attorney so you can understand your rights and how the process works in your state.

You can choose to contest the grounds for the divorce and refuse to agree to the divorce itself. You can also choose not to contest or argue with the grounds and can instead focus on all the decisions that need to be made – alimony, property settlement, custody, and support.

In many cases, it is a good idea to consider mediation as an alternative to having your case progress through the court. In fact, more and more courts require mediation before the parties' disputes will be heard. A mediator acts as a neutral third party and helps you and your spouse reach agreements and compromises to settle all of the issues in a divorce. You might also consider collaborative lawyers.

ALIMONY AND FAULT

Alimony, also referred to as *maintenance* or *spousal support*, is payment the court orders one spouse to make to another after the end of the marriage. It is usually set up to occur on a regular basis, similar to child support, but periodic lump sum payments could be the format. Sometimes the purpose of alimony is to assist one spouse in becoming financially independent. Other times the purpose of it is to create an ongoing property settlement.

Occasionally the amount of alimony a court orders is influenced by fault – which spouse *caused* the marriage to end or did something wrong to the other spouse. So, if your spouse uses your sexual orientation as a reason for the end of the marriage, this could be used to influence the court to require you to pay alimony, or to pay a higher amount of alimony than you would have had to otherwise. It can also be used as a reason to deny your alimony if you are the one asking for it.

In this kind of situation, you need an experienced lawyer, who will make sure the court understands that sexual orientation should not be a fault issue.

CUSTODY

If you have children with your spouse, the court will decide where they will primarily live and how they will divide their time between the two of you. Most states do not allow custody to be decided or influenced based on the parents' sexual orientation, however, there are some judges for whom this may be an unspoken factor. If you believe that sexual orientation is being used as a tactic in your custody case, get a lawyer who is experienced in handling these issues.

You have an absolute right to seek custody or primary residence of your children. These determinations should always be made based on what is best for the child; however, Alabama, Michigan, Missouri and Virginia have presumptions against gay parents. This means a judge presumes that being gay is a negative factor when considering custody.

Custody, in general, is decided by the *best interests* analysis. The court must decide what would be in the best interest of the children – what arrangement would benefit them the most. The rights of the parents are a secondary concern and the interest of the children is supposed to be the primary consideration.

When considering cases in which one parent is GLBT and the other parent is trying to use that as a reason for denying custody or visitation, most states use what is called a *nexus test* or *adverse impact test*. They only consider sexual orientation in a custody case if it is shown that there is a clear connection between the parent's actions and harm to the child. This means that sexuality is considered only if it has negatively impacted the child, for example, if the gay parent took the child to gay bars, frequently had many different overnight partners who interacted with the child, or performed sexual behavior in front of the child. (See the California case, *In re Marriage of Birdsall*, 197 Cal. App. 3d (1998) for an example.) It is important to note that most courts apply this adverse impact test to gay as well as straight parents. The rule is not just about how gay sexuality impacts parenting, but about how any sexuality impacts parenting.

Do not feel that you have to curtail or hide your personal life because of a custody battle. Being a good parent is the primary consideration in this kind of case. Focus on being able to demonstrate you have a stable home, good parenting skills, and a close relationship with your child. Having a loving relationship with a person of the same sex or dating people of the same sex does not impact your ability to be a good parent, period. If you are having a hard time getting this message across to the court or to your lawyer, seek help from a GLBT advocacy organization (see Appendix E).

If you are living with a partner, this can be a consideration in the case, just as it would be if you had re-partnered with someone of the opposite sex. Courts are interested in the child's environment and what kind of lifestyle he or she will have with a parent. A new partner is part of that environment and can have a positive or negative effect on the case.

TG Custody Issues

Most courts approach TG custody cases in the same way as gay and lesbian custody cases. The most important consideration by the court is the best interest of the children. The adverse interest test is also used. In one Florida case (*Kantaras v. Kantaras*), a woman who transgendered into a man won custody of his children. You can read about it at: **www.courttv.com/trials /kantaras**.

VISITATION

Part of a custody determination is a determination about *visitation*, also called *access* or *parenting time* in many states (because no one *visits* their

RAINBOW TIP

Support for children of GLBT parents:
- COLAGE (An international support organization for children of GLBT parents)
  3543 18th ST #1
  San Francisco, CA 94110
  415-861-KIDS (5437)
  www.colage.org
- *Our House* is a PBS-made video for kids about having GLBT parents. You can get more information about it at: www.itvs.org/ourhouse.
- A list of books for kids with GLBT characters can be found at: www.geocities.com/WestHollywoo d/1769/books.htm

RAINBOW TIP

Tips for Talking to Your Kids
About Being Gay

- give your child the information at a level he or she is able to understand;
- encourage questions;
- help your child see that being gay, or having a gay parent is nothing to be embarrassed or ashamed about;
- explain that being gay has nothing to do with how much you love your child and does not change your relationship;
- help your child see that being gay is about more than just sex;
- maintain a sense of humor and an approachable attitude;
- help your child understand that bias against gays exists and help him or her find ways to deal with it;
- explain that just because you are gay, it does not mean that he or she is or will be;
- explain why derogatory or incorrect statements about members of the GLBT community are wrong and why people try to spread that kind of mis-information; and,
- emphasize that you are still the same parent and this is something that has always been a part of you—you are just talking about it now.

children). If your child will not be living primarily with you, you are entitled to have time with your child. Parenting time can be divided in many, many ways and can be customized to fit your schedule, your child's needs and other factors. (Chapter 12 has more information about parenting schedules.)

Sexual orientation should not be used as a determining factor in setting up parenting time (although once again, some judges are prejudiced). Being gay should have nothing to do with how much time you spend with your child. Some spouses try to place restrictions on parenting time, by suggesting the child should not have contact with the gay non-custodial parent's friends or new partners. The only consideration that should come into play is what is best for the child. In almost all circumstances, children should have access to and time with both parents.

Unfortunately, sexual orientation is still used whether explicitly or through personal prejudices of the ruling judge to restrict custody and visitation to gay parents. Each state is different, and in fact, different courts within a state may vary widely in their attitudes in this area. The Human Rights Campaign tracks custody and visitation decisions and states that twenty-one states and the District of Columbia have good records in this area. Nine states have decisively bad records of discrimination while the remaining states are either mixed or it is unclear how their courts will rule. Log on to **www.hrc.org/familynet** to find a link to see where your state ranks.

TALKING TO YOUR KIDS ABOUT BEING GAY

It should be your decision when and how to tell your kids you are gay. Hopefully, you and the other parent can agree to this. If your kids have been told by someone else, you will still want to take the time to explain things from your point of view and help them understand who you are and what it means. (See Chapter 12 for more information on parenting issues.)

CONCLUSION

While the rights of gays are still limited, this is a time of great change, with more and more recognition and support becoming available. The GLBT community has become a powerful force and more change is on the way. Understanding your rights today will help you navigate the system and identify where more changes need to be made.

GLOSSARY

A

adoption. Legal process through which two people who were not previously in a parent-child relationship to each other become parent and child.

advanced directive. Another name for a health care directive.

adverse interest test. Method in which a court can consider a parent's sexual orientation in a custody case.

alien. Any person who is physically present in the U.S. but not a U.S. citizen or a U.S. national.

alien registration card (green card). Proof of lawful, permanent United States resident status.

alimony. Payment made by one former spouse to another after dissolution of a marriage.

American's with Disability Act (ADA). A federal law that prohibits discrimination against persons with disabilities.

arbitration. An alternative to the court system in which an arbitrator hears both sides and decides what the resolution of the dispute should be.

attorney in fact. Under a power of attorney, the person who is designated to transact business for, or make decisions for the maker. A legal agent, but not to be confused with an attorney at law.

autopsy. Medical examination of a body after death to determine cause of death.

B

beneficiary. Person who receives payment on a life insurance policy after the insured person dies.

bi-national. An immigration term referring to couples each having a different country of origin or citizenship.

C

civil union. A life partnership between two people of the same sex, similar to marriage, under Vermont law.

child support. Payment made by one parent to another after divorce or dissolution of a partnership which is intended to help provide financial support for the child.

coercive partner notification. A practice where partners are notified against the will of a patient regarding a health condition, usually relating to sexually transmitted diseases.

collaborative law. An alternative dispute resolution technique where attorneys work in a cooperative fashion, instead of as adversaries, to make decisions regarding such issues as property division and issues concerning children without involving a court.

commitment ceremony. Celebration of a life partnership.

Consolidated Omnibus Budget Reconciliation Act (COBRA). A federal law making health insurance available to employees for a period of time after leaving a job.

D

deed. Legal document creating ownership in real property.

declaration. Another name for a health care directive.

discrimination. Legal term meaning being denied rights or treated unfairly because of membership in a minority group.

dissolution. Ending an agreement or partnership.

domestic partnership. Life partnership for those not permitted to marry.

domestic partnership agreement. A contract which may or may not be legally enforceable detailing the obligations and promises a life couple makes to each other.

durable power of attorney. Power of attorney that becomes effective immediately and remains in effect indefinitely.

E

egg nuclear transfer. Cutting edge technology in which DNA is implanted into a human egg cell.

Equal Access Law of 1984. Federal law that requires public schools that receive federal funding to allow student-led clubs in public high schools to organize and meet on school property and receive equal support as other clubs so long as the organization is a student-led, special interest, non-curriculum club must.

executor. Person named in a will who is responsible for carrying out its instructions.

F

Family Medical Leave Act (FMLA). Federal law that requires employers with 50 or more employees to give 12 weeks of unpaid leave for certain medical and family situations to its employees, and guarantees a job upon return.

Federal Employment Non-Discrimination Act. Federal law prohibiting discrimination in employment but does not include sexual orientation in its protected class of people.

Federal Equal Opportunity Credit Act. Federal law prohibiting discrimination in the extension of credit, but does not include sexual orientation in its protected class of people.

Federal Fair Housing Act. Federal law providing protection from housing discrimination, but does not include sexual orientation in its protected class of people.

Federal Funeral Rule. Federal law, enforced by the Federal Trade Commission, that requires that information regarding funeral pricing be accurate and itemized, and prohibits the provider of funeral services from making misrepresentations of the law and other harmful practices.

foster care. Situation in which a person accepts a child into his or her home and cares for him on a temporary basis on behalf of the state because the legal parent is unable to or is not permitted to.

G

gay straight alliance (GSA). School support group of children of GLBT families or gay teens.

gender identity disorder (GID). A classification by the American Psychiatric Association of transgender individuals.

gift tax. Federal tax imposed on gifts made to someone other than your spouse with a value over $11,000 in any one calendar year.

guaranteed insurability rider. Addition to a life insurance policy that allows you to purchase more insurance without going through medical history or exams.

guaranteed issue life insurance. Life insurance that is offered regardless of a person's risk of death.

guardian. Person who is chosen by a court to care for a child after his or her legal parent has died.

H

health care directive. A document indicating choices you have made about your own health care and/or appointing someone to make medical decisions for you, should you be unable to.

health care power of attorney. A legal document appointing a person to make medical decisions for you should become unable, a type of health care directive.

health care proxy. A legal document appointing a person to make medical decisions for you should become unable, a type of health care directive.

Health Insurance Portability and Accountability Act (HIPAA). A federal law controlling health insurance eligibility.

holographic will. Handwritten will.

I

immigrant. Any person who has been granted lawful permanent residence status.

immigration. Process through which people legally enter the United States and get permission to remain.

Immigration Act of 1990. Federal law updating the United States immigration policies with a significant change in the number of work visas allowed per year.

Immigration and Naturalization Service (INS). The U.S. government agency responsible for administering laws and regulations regarding non-U.S. citizens entering and remaining in the United States.

impaired risk life insurance. Life insurance for people with a higher risk of death

imputed income. Term used to describe the value of goods or services received that is added to an employee's income for tax purposes. Seen in situations where one partner receives benefits from the other partner's employer (insurance or other fringe benefits). The IRS requires the value of the benefits received be added to the employee's gross income.

income shifting. Transferring income from one person to another in a lower income tax bracket.

insemination. Medical process in which sperm is inserted by a doctor into a woman's uterus or fallopian tubes in the hopes of creating a pregnancy.

intestate. Dying without a will.

J

joint annuitant. A equal co-owner of an annuity.

joint legal custody. Where custody of a child is held equally by both parents regardless of where the child actually physically resides. This gives the parent with whom the child does not primarily resides full decision making authority over matters concerning the child.

joint tenancy. Manner in which to own property whereby two people each own an equal interest, and ownership passes at the death of one owner to the other owner, not through the decedent's estate.

joint tenants with right of survivorship. Type of ownership in real property where the ownership in the property passes to the surviving owner when one owner dies.

L

Lambda Legal. An organization committed to achieving full recognition of the civil rights of GLBT members and people with HIV or AIDS through impact litigation, education, and public policy work.

landlord. Person who owns real property and rents it to others.

legal custody. Custody which grants a parent the right to make ultimate decisions regarding matters concerning his or her child.

living trust. Legal document transferring ownership in assets or belongings while you are still alive.

living will. Type of legal document detailing what medical procedures you consent to should you become unable to make decisions.

M

maintenance. *See alimony.*

Matthew Shepard. A 21-year old college student who was murdered in an anti-gay hate crime in Laramie, Wyoming, sparking a wave of anti-hate crime protesting.

mediation. A process in which a third party neutral assists people in reaching a resolution to a dispute.

Medicaid. Governmental program that provides payment for medical service to persons who cannot otherwise afford health care.

Medical Information Bureau (MIB). A database checked by life insurance underwriters to obtain health information about people applying for life insurance.

Megan's Law. The term used to describe statutes requiring local law enforcement agencies to notify a community of any resident convicted of a sexually related crime. Named after Megan Kanka, who at age seven, was raped and murdered by a twice-convicted sex offender.

N

nexus test. Method in which a court can consider a parent's sexual orientation in a custody case.

no-fault divorce. Concept accepted by most states which allows a couple to divorce without the need for stating a formal reason for the marital breakdown.

O

organ donor agreement. A written document outline a person's wishes that his or her organs be donated after their death to another or science.

P

palimony. Court ordered support paid by one member of a couple, who were never married, to the other after a break-up.

parenting time. *See visitation.*

Permanent Partners Immigration Act (PPIA). A proposed bill which would change current U.S. immigration law and allow United States citizens and lawful permanent residents to sponsor their permanent partners for residence in the United States.

physical custody. Term used to describe the parent with whom a child primarily resides.

power of attorney (POA). Legal document giving someone else the authority to manage your business, financial and legal affairs for you.

probate. Court process in which is a will is a validated and an estate is distributed.

psychological parent. Person that a child thinks of and relates to as if he or she were a parent.

R

real property. Real estate, land/buildings.

residential custody. Term used to describe the parent with whom a child primarily resides.

revocable trust. A trust, such as a living trust, the maker of which has full right and ability to change, amend, or revoke.

right of survivorship. Term specifically required by some states to be included in the title of property held in joint tenancy to indicate that the property passes on death to the joint owner outside of probate.

S

second parent adoption. Adoption situation where a partner adopts the child of his or her partner.

sex reassignment. Gender change.

sexually transmitted disease (STD). A disease that is spread through sexual contact between two people.

sodomy. Defined as oral or anal intercourse; illegal in some states.

spousal support. *See alimony.*

springing power of attorney. Power of attorney that takes effect only upon the happening of an event, such an illness.

successor trustee. A trustee named in a trust document that only takes power upon a previously named trustee being unable to perform.

surrogacy. An arrangement whereby a woman carries a child for another person or another couple.

T

tenant. Person renting real property.

tenants in common. A manner to hold property between two or more individuals. Each owner's share is based on his or her portion of ownership and does not transfer to the other owners automatically at death, but instead is part of a decedent's estate.

Totten trust. A revocable trust established by depositing money in one's own name as trustee for another, with the usual goal to avoid probate over the property.

transgender (TG). Person who changes gender through medical and psychological treatment.

trustee. A person named in a trust document who has legal title to the property contained therein, but holds and manages it for the benefit of the trust maker.

U

umbrella policy. An insurance policy that provides coverage over the basic amount provided in a liability policy.

Uniform Transfers on Death Securities Registration Act. An act allowing investment or other accounts is to be re-registered on request after the owner's death in the name of a beneficiary.

U.S. citizen. A person born in the U.S., or born outside the U.S. to a U.S. citizen parent, or a person naturalized.

V

visa. Legal document that permits entry into a country.

visitation. Term used to refer to the amount of time a non-custodial parent spends with his or her child after a divorce.

viatical settlements. Term used to refer to the practice of selling a life insurance policy to a company who makes an immediate cash payment, but then becomes the beneficiary of the proceeds from the policy at your death.

W

will. Legal document detailing how you wish to distribute your belongings after your death.

-Appendix A-
VERMONT
CIVIL UNION LAW

Title 15: Domestic Relations
Chapter 23: Civil Unions
Section 1201. Definitions
As used in this chapter:
(1) "Certificate of civil union" means a document that certifies that the persons named on the certificate have established a civil union in this state in compliance with this chapter and 18 V.S.A. chapter 106.
(2) "Civil union" means that two eligible persons have established a relationship pursuant to this chapter, and may receive the benefits and protections and be subject to the responsibilities of spouses.
(3) "Commissioner" means the commissioner of health.
(4) "Marriage" means the legally recognized union of one man and one woman.
(5) "Party to a civil union" means a person who has established a civil union pursuant to this chapter and 18 V.S.A. chapter 106. (Added 1999, No. 91 (Adj. Sess.), Section 3.)

Section 1202. Requisites of a valid civil union
For a civil union to be established in Vermont, it shall be necessary that the parties to a civil union satisfy all of the following criteria:
(1) Not be a party to another civil union or a marriage.
(2) Be of the same sex and therefore excluded from the marriage laws of this state.
(3) Meet the criteria and obligations set forth in 18 V.S.A. chapter 106. (Added 1999, No. 91 (Adj. Sess.), Section 3.)

Section 1203. Person shall not enter a civil union with a relative

(a) A woman shall not enter a civil union with her mother, grandmother, daughter, granddaughter, sister, brother's daughter, sister's daughter, father's sister or mother's sister.

(b) A man shall not enter a civil union with his father, grandfather, son, grandson, brother, brother's son, sister's son, father's brother or mother's brother.

(c) A civil union between persons prohibited from entering a civil union in subsection (a) or (b) of this section is void. (Added 1999, No. 91 (Adj. Sess.), Section 3.)

Section 1204. BENEFITS, PROTECTIONS AND RESPONSIBILITIES OF PARTIES TO A CIVIL UNION

(a) Parties to a civil union shall have all the same benefits, protections and responsibilities under law, whether they derive from statute, administrative or court rule, policy, common law or any other source of civil law, as are granted to spouses in a marriage.

(b) A party to a civil union shall be included in any definition or use of the terms "spouse," "family," "immediate family," "dependent," "next of kin," and other terms that denote the spousal relationship, as those terms are used throughout the law.

(c) Parties to a civil union shall be responsible for the support of one another to the same degree and in the same manner as prescribed under law for married persons.

(d) The law of domestic relations, including annulment, separation and divorce, child custody and support, and property division and maintenance shall apply to parties to a civil union.

(e) The following is a nonexclusive list of legal benefits, protections and responsibilities of spouses, which shall apply in like manner to parties to a civil union:

(1) laws relating to title, tenure, descent and distribution, intestate succession, waiver of will, survivorship, or other incidents of the acquisition,

ownership, or transfer, inter vivos or at death, of real or personal property, including eligibility to hold real and personal property as tenants by the entirety (parties to a civil union meet the common law unity of person qualification for purposes of a tenancy by the entirety);

(2) causes of action related to or dependent upon spousal status, including an action for wrongful death, emotional distress, loss of consortium, dramshop, or other torts or actions under contracts reciting, related to, or dependent upon spousal status;

(3) probate law and procedure, including nonprobate transfer;

(4) adoption law and procedure;

(5) group insurance for state employees under 3 V.S.A. Section 631, and continuing care contracts under 8 V.S.A. Section 8005;

(6) spouse abuse programs under 3 V.S.A. Section 18;

(7) prohibitions against discrimination based upon marital status;

(8) victim's compensation rights under 13 V.S.A. Section 5351;

(9) workers' compensation benefits;

(10) laws relating to emergency and nonemergency medical care and treatment, hospital visitation and notification, including the Patient's Bill of Rights under 18 V.S.A. chapter 42 and the Nursing Home Residents' Bill of Rights under 33 V.S.A. chapter 73;

(11) terminal care documents under 18 V.S.A. chapter 111, and durable power of attorney for health care execution and revocation under 14 V.S.A. chapter 121;

(12) family leave benefits under 21 V.S.A. chapter 5, subchapter 4A;

(13) public assistance benefits under state law;

(14) laws relating to taxes imposed by the state or a municipality other than estate taxes;

(15) laws relating to immunity from compelled testimony and the marital communication privilege;

(16) the homestead rights of a surviving spouse under 27 V.S.A. Section 105 and homestead property tax allowance under 32 V.S.A. Section 6062;

(17) laws relating to loans to veterans under 8 V.S.A. Section 1849;

(18) the definition of family farmer under 10 V.S.A. Section 272;

(19) laws relating to the making, revoking and objecting to anatomical gifts by others under 18 V.S.A. Section 5240;

(20) state pay for military service under 20 V.S.A. Section 1544;

(21) application for early voter absentee ballot under 17 V.S.A. Section 2532;

(22) family landowner rights to fish and hunt under 10 V.S.A. Section 4253;

(23) legal requirements for assignment of wages under 8 V.S.A. Section 2235; and

(24) affirmance of relationship under 15 V.S.A. Section 7.

(f) The rights of parties to a civil union, with respect to a child of whom either becomes the natural parent during the term of the civil union, shall be the same as those of a married couple, with respect to a child of whom either spouse becomes the natural parent during the marriage. (Added 1999, No. 91 (Adj. Sess.), Section 3.)

Section 1205. Modification of civil union terms

Parties to a civil union may modify the terms, conditions, or effects of their civil union in the same manner and to the same extent as married persons who execute an antenuptial agreement or other agreement recognized and enforceable under the law, setting forth particular understandings with respect to their union. (Added 1999, No. 91 (Adj. Sess.), Section 3.)

Section 1206. Dissolution of civil unions

The family court shall have jurisdiction over all proceedings relating to the dissolution of civil unions. The dissolution of civil unions shall follow the same procedures and be subject to the same substantive rights and obligations that are involved in the dissolution of marriage in accordance with chapter 11 of this title, including any residency requirements. (Added 1999, No. 91 (Adj. Sess.), Section 3.)

Section 1207. Commissioner of health; duties

(a) The commissioner shall provide civil union license and certificate forms to all town and county clerks.

(b) The commissioner shall keep a record of all civil unions. (Added 1999, No. 91 (Adj. Sess.), Section 3.)

TITLE 18: HEALTH

Chapter 106: Civil Union; Records And Licenses

Section 5160. Issuance of civil union license; certification; return of civil union certificate

(a) Upon application in a form prescribed by the department, a town clerk shall issue a civil union license in the form prescribed by the department, and shall enter thereon the names of the parties to the proposed civil union, fill out the form as far as practicable and retain a copy in the clerk's office. At least one party to the proposed civil union shall sign the application attesting to the accuracy of the facts stated. The license shall be issued by the clerk of the town where either party resides or, if neither is a resident of the state, by any town clerk in the state.

(b) A civil union license shall be delivered by one of the parties to a proposed civil union, within 60 days from the date of issue, to a person authorized to certify civil unions by section 5164 of this title. If the proposed civil union is not certified within 60 days from the date of issue, the license shall become void. After a person has certified the civil union, he or she shall fill out that part of the form on the license provided for such use, sign and certify the civil union. Thereafter, the document shall be known as a civil union certificate.

(c) Within ten days of the certification, the person performing the certification shall return the civil union certificate to the office of the town clerk from which the license was issued. The town clerk shall retain and file the original according to sections 5007 and 5008 of this title.

(d) A town clerk who knowingly issues a civil union license upon application of a person residing in another town in the state, or a county clerk who knowingly issues a civil union license upon application of a person other than as provided in section 5005 of this title, or a clerk who issues such a license without first requiring the applicant to fill out, sign and make oath to the declaration contained therein as provided in section 5160 of this title, shall be fined not more than $50.00 nor less than $20.00.

(e) A person making application to a clerk for a civil union license who makes a material misrepresentation in the declaration of intention shall be deemed guilty of perjury.

(f) A town clerk shall provide a person who applies for a civil union license with information prepared by the secretary of state that advises such person of the benefits, protections and responsibilities of a civil union and that Vermont residency may be required for dissolution of a civil union in Vermont. (Added 1999, No. 91 (Adj. Sess.), Section 5.)

Section 5161. Issuance of license

(a) A town clerk shall issue a civil union license to all applicants who have complied with the provisions of section 5160 of this title, and who are otherwise qualified under the laws of the state to apply for a civil union license.

(b) An assistant town clerk may perform the duties of a town clerk under this chapter. (Added 1999, No. 91 (Adj. Sess.), Section 5.)

Section 5162. Proof of legal qualifications of parties to a civil union; penalty

(a) Before issuing a civil union license to an applicant, the town clerk shall be confident, through presentation of affidavits or other proof, that each party to the intended civil union meets the criteria set forth to enter into a civil union.

(b) Affidavits shall be in a form prescribed by the board, and shall be attached to and filed with the civil union certificate in the office of the clerk of the town wherein the license was issued.

(c) A clerk who fails to comply with the provisions of this section, or who issues a civil union license with knowledge that either or both of the parties to a civil union have failed to comply with the requirements of the laws of this state, or a person who, having authority and having such knowledge, certifies such a civil union, shall be fined not more than $100.00. (Added 1999, No. 91 (Adj. Sess.), Section 5.)

Section 5163. Restrictions as to minors and incompetent persons

(a) A clerk shall not issue a civil union license when either party to the intended civil union is:

    (1) under 18 years of age;

    (2) non compos mentis;

    (3) under guardianship, without the written consent of such guardian.

(b) A clerk who knowingly violates subsection (a) of this section shall be fined not more than $20.00. A person who aids in procuring a civil union license by falsely pretending to be the guardian having authority to give consent to the civil union shall be fined not more than $500.00. (Added 1999, No. 91 (Adj. Sess.), Section 5.)

Section 5164. Persons authorized to certify civil unions

Civil unions may be certified by a supreme court justice, a superior court judge, a district judge, a judge of probate, an assistant judge, a justice of the peace or by a member of the clergy residing in this state and ordained or licensed, or otherwise regularly authorized by the published laws or discipline of the general conference, convention or other authority of his or her faith or denomination or by such a clergy person residing in an adjoining state or country, whose parish, church, temple, mosque or other religious organization lies wholly or in part in this state, or by a member of the clergy residing in some other state of the United States or in the Dominion of Canada, provided he or she has first secured from the probate court of the district within which the civil union is to be certified, a special authorization, authorizing him or her to certify the civil union if such probate judge determines that the circumstances make the special authorization desirable. Civil unions among the Friends or Quakers, the Christadelphian Ecclesia and the Baha'i Faith may be certified in the manner used in such societies. (Added 1999, No. 91 (Adj. Sess.), Section 5.)

Section 5165. Civil union license required for certification; failure to return

(a) Persons authorized by section 5164 of this title to certify civil unions shall require a civil union license of the parties before certifying the civil union. The license shall afford full immunity to the person who certifies the civil union.

(b) A person who certifies a civil union shall be fined not less than $10.00, if such person:

      (1) certifies a civil union without first obtaining the license; or

      (2) fails to properly fill out the license and, within ten days from the date of the certification, return the license and certificate of civil union to the clerk's office from which it was issued. (Added 1999, No. 91 (Adj. Sess.), Section 5.)

Section 5166. Certification by unauthorized person; penalty; validity of civil unions

(a) An unauthorized person who knowingly undertakes to join others in a civil union shall be imprisoned not more than six months or fined not more than $300.00 nor less than $100.00, or both.

(b) A civil union certified before a person falsely professing to be a justice or a member of the clergy shall be valid, provided that the civil union is in other respects lawful, and that either of the parties to a civil union believed that he or she was lawfully joined in a civil union. (Added 1999, No. 91 (Adj. Sess.), Section 5.)

Section 5167. Evidence of civil union

A copy of the record of the civil union received from the town or county clerk, the commissioner of health or the director of public records shall be presumptive evidence of the civil union in all courts. (Added 1999, No. 91 (Adj. Sess.), Section 5.)

Section 5168. Correction of civil union certificate

(a) Within six months after a civil union is certified, the town clerk may correct or complete a civil union certificate, upon application by a party to a civil union or by the person who certified the civil union. The town clerk shall certify that such correction or completion was made pursuant to this section and note the date. The town clerk may refuse an application for correction or completion; in which case, the applicant may petition the probate court for such correction or completion.

(b) After six months from the date a civil union is certified, a civil union certificate may only be corrected or amended pursuant to decree of the probate court in the district where the original certificate is filed.

(c) The probate court shall set a time for a hearing and, if the court deems necessary, give notice of the time and place by posting such information in the probate court office. After a hearing, the court shall make findings with respect to the correction of the civil union certificate as are supported by the evidence. The court shall issue a decree setting forth the facts as found, and transmit a certified copy of the decree to the supervisor of vital records registration. The supervisor of vital records registration shall transmit the same to the appropriate town clerk to amend the original or issue a new certificate. The words "Court Amended" shall be typed, written or stamped at the top of the new or amended certificate with the date of the decree and the name of the issuing court. (Added 1999, No. 91 (Adj. Sess.), Section 5.)

Section 5169. Delayed certificates of civil union

(a) Persons who were parties to a certified civil union ceremony in this state for whom no certificate of civil union was filed, as required by law, may petition the probate court of the district in which the civil union license was obtained to determine the facts, and to order the issuance of a delayed certificate of civil union.

(b) The probate court shall set a time for hearing on the petition and, if the court deems necessary, give notice of the time and place by posting such information in the probate court office. After hearing proper and relevant evidence as may be presented, the court shall make findings with respect to the civil union as are supported by the evidence.

(c) The court shall issue a decree setting forth the facts as found, and transmit a certified copy of said facts to the supervisor of vital records registration.

(d) Where a delayed certificate is to be issued, the supervisor of vital records registration shall prepare a delayed certificate of civil union, and transmit it, with the decree, to the clerk of the town where the civil union license was issued. This delayed certificate shall have the word "Delayed" printed at the top, and shall certify that the certificate was ordered by a court pursuant to this chapter, with the date of the decree. The town clerk shall file the delayed certificate and, in accordance with the provisions of section 5010 of this title, furnish a copy to the department of health.

(e) Town clerks receiving new certificates in accordance with this section shall file and index them in the most recent book of civil unions, and also index them with civil unions occurring at the same time. (Added 1999, No. 91 (Adj. Sess.), Section 5.)

–Appendix B–
VERMONT
TOWN CLERK LIST

To legalize a civil union in Vermont, a civil union license must be obtained. This can be done in person or by mail. If you or your partner live in Vermont, you must go to your town clerk. If you do not live in Vermont, you can submit your application to any Vermont town clerk. This appendix lists the Vermont town clerks, gives their mailing addresses, telephone numbers, and hours of operation.

ADDISON
Jane B. Grace
7099 VT RTE 22A
Addison, VT 05491
802-759-2020
M-F 8:30-12 & 1-4:30

ALBANY
Debra Ann Geoffroy
P.O. Box 284
Albany, VT 05820
802-755-6100
T Th 9-4; W 9-7
albany@pop.state.vt.us

ALBURG
Barbara W. Baker
P.O. Box 346
Alburg, VT 05440
802-796-3468
M-F 9-12 & 1-5

ANDOVER
Paul R. Disney
953 Weston-Andover Rd.
Andover, VT 05143
802-875-2765
M,T,Th,F 9-1; W 11-3

ARLINGTON

Joyce A. Wyman
P.O. Box 304
Arlington, VT 05250
802-375-2332
M-F 9-2
arltc@adelphia.net

ATHENS

Darlene Wyman
25 Brookline Road
Athens, VT 05143
802-869-3370
M 9-1; or by appt.
athens@tax.state.vt.us

BAKERSFIELD

Joyce Morin
P.O. Box 203
Bakersfield, VT 05441
802-827-4495
M-F 9-12

BALTIMORE

Judith A. Thomas, CMC
1902 Baltimore Rd.
Baltimore, VT 05143
802-263-5274
S 10-12; evenings by appt.

BARNARD

Diane L. Rainey
P.O. Box 274
Barnard, VT 05031
802-234-9211
M,T,W 8-3:30

BARNET

William E. Hoar
P. O. Box 15
Barnet, VT 05821
802-633-2256
M-F 9-12 & 1-4:30
barnet@connriver.net

BARRE CITY

Eugene G. Stratton
P. O. Box 418
Barre, VT 05641
802-476-0242
M-F 8:30-5
Estratton@
citygov.ci.barre.vt.us

BARRE TOWN

Donna Kelty
P.O. Box 124
Websterville, VT 05678
802-479-9391
M-F 8-4:30
dkelty@barretown.org

BARTON

Katherine H. White
P. O. Box 657
Barton, VT 05822
802-525-6222
M-F 8:30-5
barton@tax.state.vt.us

BELVIDERE
Shirley Brown
3996 VT RTE 109
Belvidere, VT 05442
802-644-6621
T,W,Th 8:30-3:30
lands@mt-mansfield.com

BENNINGTON
Timothy R. Corcoran
205 South Street
Bennington, VT 05201
802-442-1043
M-F 8-5
benclerk@sover.net

BENSON
Janet Ladd
P. O. Box 163
Benson, VT 05731
802-537-2611
M,T,W,Th 9-12 & 1-4:30
benson@tax.state.vt.us

BERKSHIRE
Virginia M. Messier
4454 Watertower Road
Enosburg Falls, VT 05450
802-933-2335
M,T,Th,F 9-12 & 1-4;
W 9-12

BERLIN
Rosemary Morse
108 Shed Road
Berlin, VT 05602
802-229-9298
M-F 8:30-4:30

BETHEL
Jean Burnham
RR 2, Box 85
Bethel, VT 05032
802-234-9722
M & Th 8-12:30 & 1-4;
T & F 8-12
bethel@together.net

BLOOMFIELD
Paulette Routhier
P. O. Box 336
N. Stratford, NH 03590
802-962-5191
T & Th 9-3
bloomfield@tax.state.vt.us

BOLTON
Deborah LaRiviere
3045 T. Roosevelt Hwy.
Bolton, VT 05676
802-434-5075
M,T,W,Th 7-4
dlariviere53@yahoo.com

BRADFORD

Louise M. Allen
P.O. Box 339
Bradford, VT 05033
802-222-4728
M-F 8:30-4:30
bradclrk@sover.net

BRAINTREE

Cora L. Benoir
932 Vt. Rt. 12A
Braintree, VT 05060
802-728-9787
T,Th 8-12 & 1-5 W 1-5
braintreeclerk@innevi.com

BRANDON

William A. Dick
49 Center Street
Brandon, VT 05733
802-247-5721
M-F 8-4
wadick@sover.net

BRATTLEBORO

Annette L. Capp
230 Main St., Suite 108
Brattleboro, VT 05301
802-254-4541 ext129
M-F 8:30-5
acappy@brattleboro.org

BRIDGEWATER

Nancy Robinson
P.O. Box 14
Bridgewater, VT 05034
802-672-3334
M-Th 8-4;F 8-12
twnbridg@sover.net

BRIDPORT

Valerie Bourgeois
P.O. Box 27
Bridport, VT 05734
802-758-2483
M,T,F 9-4; W 9-12 & 1-4;
Th 9-12

BRIGHTON

Lucille Stevens
P. O. Box 377
Island Pond, VT 05846
802-723-4405
M-F 8-3:30

BRISTOL

Penny Sherwood
P.O. Box 249
Bristol, VT 05443
802-453-2486
M-F 8:00-4:30
bristoltown@gmavt.net

BROOKFIELD
Jane B. Woodfuff
P.O. Box 463
Brookfield, VT 05036
802-276-3352
M & Th 8:30-12 & 1-4:30;
T & F 8:30-12; Closed W
Btownhall@aol.com

BROOKLINE
Penny Harrington
P.O. Box 403
Newfane, VT 05345
802-365-4648
W 9-2;1st S of month 9-12
brookline@tax.state.vt.us

BROWNINGTON
Cheryl Perry
509 Dutton Brook Lane
Brownington, VT 05860
802-754-8401
M 9-12; W 9-12 & 1-3:30;
Th 9-12
brownington@tax.state.vt.us

BRUNSWICK
Sharon B. Graham
994 VT Rt. 102
Brunswick, VT 05905
802-962-5514
By appt.
brunswick@tax.state.vt.us

BURKE
Priscilla Aldrich, CVC/CVT
212 School Street
W. Burke, VT 05871
802-467-3717
M-F 8-4
burke@kingcon.com

BURLINGTON
Brendan S. Keleher, CAO
149 Church Street
Burlington, VT 05401
802-865-7019
M 8-7:30; T-F 8-4:30
bkeleher@ci.burlington.vt.us

CABOT
Patricia diStefano
P.O. Box 36
Cabot, VT 05647
802-563-2279
M 9-6; T Th 9-5; W 12-5;
F 9-1
tcocabot@pivot.net

CALAIS
Eva M. Morse
668 West County Road
Calais, VT 05648
802-223-5952
M,T,Th 8-5; S 8-12

CAMBRIDGE

Jane N. Porter
P.O. Box 127
Jeffersonville, VT 05464
802-644-2251
M-F 8-4
cambridgevt@pwshift.com

CANAAN

Linda L. Hikel
P.O. Box 159
Canaan, VT 05903
802-266-3370
M-F 9-3
canaan@sover.net

CASTLETON

Ellen P. LaFleche
P.O. Box 727
Castleton, VT 05735
802-468-2212
M-F 8-12 & 1-4
casclerk@shoreham.net

CAVENDISH

Jane S. Pixley
P.O. Box 126
Cavendish, VT 05142
802-226-7291 or 7292
M,Th,F 9-12 & 1-5; W 9-12
& 1-6; T 9-12 & 1-4:30

CHARLESTON

Jeannine Bennett
5063 Vt. Rte. 105
W. Charleston, VT 05872
802-895-2814
M,T,Th F 8-3
charleston@surfglobal.net

CHARLOTTE

Mary A. Mead
P.O. Box 119
Charlotte, VT 05445
802-425-3071
M-F 8-4
mary@townofcharlotte.com

CHELSEA

Diane Mattoon
P.O. Box 266
Chelsea, VT 05038
802-685-4460
M-W 8-12 & 1-4
dmattoon@innevi.com

CHESTER

Sandra K. Walker
P.O. Box 370
Chester, VT 05143
802-875-2173
M-F 8-5

CHITTENDEN

Roberta Janoski
P. O. Box 89
Chittenden, VT 05737
802-483-6647
M,T,Th,F 1:30-5 W 1:30-7
slabcity@together.net

CLARENDON

Joyce A. Pedone
P.O. Box 30
Clarendon, VT 05759
802-775-4274
M-Th 10-4
vtdrifters@aol.com

COLCHESTER

Karen Richard
P.O. Box 55
Colchester, VT 05446
802-654-0727
M-F 8-4
colchester@tax.state.vt.us

CONCORD

Connie Quimby
P.O. Box 317
Concord, VT 05824
802-695-2220
M-F 7:30-3:30
conclerk@kingcon.com

CORINTH

Susan L. Fortunati
P.O. Box 461
Corinth, VT 05039
802-439-5850
M,Th,F 8:30-3; T 12-6; 1st
and last S of month 8:30-12

CORNWALL

Joan Payne
2629 Route 30
Cornwall, VT 05753
802-462-2775
T-F 12:30-4:30
cornwall@tax.state.vt.us

COVENTRY

Peggy J. Rackleff
P.O. Box 104
Coventry, VT 05825
802-754-2288
M-Th 8-12
pjrtc@together.net

CRAFTSBURY

Yvette Brown
P.O. Box 55
Craftsbury, VT 05826
802-586-2823
T-F 8:30-4:00;
M & S by appt.
fevt@kingcon.com

DANBY
> Janice Arnold
> P.O. Box 231
> Danby, VT 05739
> 802-293-5136
> M-Th 9-12 & 1-4

DANVILLE
> Virginia W. Morse
> P.O. Box 183
> Danville, VT 05828
> 802-684-3352
> M-F 8-4

DERBY
> Nicole M. Daigle
> P.O. Box 25
> Derby, VT 05829
> 802-766-4906
> M-F 8-4
> derbytc@sover.net

DORSET
> Denise M. Veillette,
> CMC, CVC
> PO Box 0024
> E. Dorset, VT 05253
> 802-362-1178
> M-F 9-2 & by appt.
> vtclerk057@juno.com

DOVER
> Mary Lou Raymo, CMC
> P.O. Box 527
> W. Dover, VT 05356
> 802-464-5100
> M-F 9-5
> doverto@sover.net

DUMMERSTON
> Janice C. Duke, CMC
> 1523 Middle Road
> E. Dummerston, VT 05346
> 802-257-1496
> M,T,Th,F 9-3; W 11-5
> dummerston@tax.state.vt.us

DUXBURY
> J. Kenneth Scott
> 3316 Crossett Hill Road
> Duxbury, VT 05676
> 802-244-6660
> M & Th 8-4; T & W 8-5
> duxbury@madriver.com

EAST HAVEN
> Franklin R. Higgins
> P.O. Box 10
> East Haven, VT 05837
> 802-467-3772
> T 2-7; Th 8-12
> easthaven@tax.state.vt.us

EAST MONTPELIER

Sylvia M. Tosi, CVC, CVT
P.O. Box 157
E. Montpelier, VT 05651
802-223-3313
M-Th 9-5; F 9-12
eastmont1@adelphia.net

EDEN

Candace Vear
71 Old Schoolhouse Rd.
Eden Mills, VT 05653
802-635-2528
M-Th 8-12:30 & 1:30-4
cvear@eden.k12.vt.us

ELMORE

Sharon Draper
P.O. Box 123
Lake Elmore, VT 05657
802-888-2637
T-W-Th 9-3
elmore@aol.com

ENOSBURGH

Carolyn Stimpson
P.O. Box 465
Enosburg Falls, VT 05450
802-933-4421
M-F 9-12 & 1-4

ESSEX

Cheryl Moomey
81 Main Street
Essex Junction, VT 05452
802-879-0413
M-F 7:30-4:30
cmoomey@essex.org

FAIR HAVEN

Suzanne Dechame
3 North Park Place
Fair Haven, VT 05743
802-265-3610
M-F 8-4
fairhven@sover.net

FAIRFAX

Tina Levick
P.O. Box 27
Fairfax, VT 05454
802-849-6111
M-F 9-4 Mon. eve. 6-8

FAIRFIELD

G. F. Longway
P.O. Box 5
Fairfield, VT 05455
802-827-3261
M-F 10-2; M eve. 7:30-8

FAIRLEE

Georgette Wolf-Ludwig,
CVC
P.O. Box 95
Fairlee, VT 05045
802-333-4363
M & T 8:30-4:30;
W 10-6 or by appt.
fairlee@tax.state.vt.us

FAYSTON

Virginia Vasseur, CVC
866 North Fayston Road
North Fayston, VT 05660
802-496-2454
M-F 9-3:30

FERRISBURGH

Jan Oosterman
P.O. Box 6
Ferrisburgh, VT 05456
802-877-3429
M-F 8-4
ferristc@together.net

FLETCHER

Elaine C. Sweet
215 Cambridge Road
Cambridge, VT 05444
802-849-6616
M 9-3:30 & 6:30-8:30; T-Th
9-3:30
townflet@together.net

FRANKLIN

Susan E. Clark
P.O. Box 82
Franklin, VT 05457
802-285-2101
M T F 9-12 & 1-4; W 9-12;
Th 9-12 & 1-7
townoff@franklinvt.net

GEORGIA

Laurie K. Broe
47 Town Common Rd,N
St. Albans, VT 05478
802-524-3524
M 11-7;T Th F 8-4
ljkbroe@yahoo.com

GLOVER

Donna Sweeney
51 Bean Hill
Glover, VT 05839
802-525-6227
M-F 8-4
glovertc@vtlink.net

GOSHEN

Madine J. Reed
50 Carlisle Hill Road
Goshen, VT 05733
802-247-6455
T 9-1; and by appt.
goshen@tax.state.vt.us

GRAFTON

Cynthia W. Gibbs
P.O. Box 180
Grafton, VT 05146
802-843-2419
M,T,Th,F 9-12 & 1-4

GRANBY

Nellie Noble
P.O. Box 56
Granby, VT 05840
802-328-3611
By appt
granby@sover.net

GRAND ISLE

Dencie Mitchell
PO Box 49
Grand Isle, VT 05458
802-372-8830
M-F 8:30-12 & 1-4:30
grandislevt@attglobal.net

GRANVILLE

Paula Roth
P.O. Box 66
Granville, VT 05747
802-767-4403
M-Th 9-3
granvilletown@gmavt.net

GREENSBORO

Bridget Collier
P.O. Box 119
Greensboro, VT 05841
802-533-2911
M-F 9-12 & 1-4:30
brideyvt@yahoo.com

GROTON

Jeanne C. Partington
314 Scott Highway
Groton, VT 05046
802-584-3276
M-Th 7-12 & 12:30-3:30

GUILDHALL

Albert H. Tetreault
P.O. Box 10
Guildhall, VT 05905
802-676-3797
T & Th 10-1 or by appt.

GUILFORD

Barbara B. Oles
236 School Road
Guilford, VT 05301
802-254-6857
M,T,Th,F 9-4; W 9-12 &
6:30-8:30pm
boles@sover.net

HALIFAX
Laura Sumner
P. O. Box 127
West Halifax, VT 05358
802-368-7390
M,T,F 9-4; S 9-12
halifax@tax.state.vt.us

HANCOCK
Linda A. Anderson
P.O. Box 100
Hancock, VT 05748
802-767-3660
M & Th 8-3; T 8-4; W 9-5
hancock@tax.state.vt.us

HARDWICK
Gerald S. Hall
P.O. Box 523
Hardwick, VT 05843
802-472-5971
M-F 9-4
hardwick@vtlink.net

HARTFORD
Mary E. Hill
171 Bridge Street
White River Jct., VT 05001
802-295-2785
M-F 8-12 & 1-5
mhill@hartford-vt.org

HARTLAND
Clyde A. Jenne
P.O. Box 349
Hartland, VT 05048
802-436-2444
M-F 8-4
hartlandvtclerk@
hotmail.com

HIGHGATE
Cora A. Baker
P.O. Box 67
Highgate Center, VT
05459
802-868-4697
M-F 8:30-12 & 1-4:30

HINESBURG
Melissa B. Ross
P.O. Box 133
Hinesburg, VT 05461
802-482-2281
M,T,Th,F 8-4; W 11-7
townclerk@gmavt.net

HOLLAND
Monica R. Yeamans,
CVC/CVT"'
120 School Road - Holland
Derby Line, VT 05830
802-895-4440
M,T,Th,F 9-2; 1st & 3rd
Mon 6:15 p.m.-7 p.m.
holland@vtlink.net

HUBBARDTON

Margaret Vittum
1831 Monument Hill Road
Castleton, VT   05735
802-273-2951
M,W,F 9-2

HUNTINGTON

Mary Juli Lax (Juli)
4930 Main Road
Huntington, VT   05462
802-434-2032
M & W 8-4; T & F 7-2;
Th 11-6
julilax@accessvt.com

HYDE PARK

Gary Anderson
P.O. Box 98
Hyde Park, VT   05655
802-888-2300
M-F 8-4
thp2300@aol.com

IRA

Ralph Preston
808 Route 133-IRA
W. Rutland, VT   05777
802-235-2745
M 9:30-2:30; T 2-7

IRASBURG

Vickie Hall
P.O. Box 51
Irasburg, VT   05845
802-754-2242
M,W,Th 9-3; T 3-6
irasburg@tax.state.vt.us

ISLE LA MOTTE

Suzanne K. LaBombard
P.O. Box 250
Isle La Motte, VT   05463
802-928-3434
T & Th 8-3 S 9-12
islemott@together.net

JAMAICA

Bonnie West
P.O. Box 173
Jamaica, VT   05343
802-874-4681
T-F 9-12 & 1-4
jamaica@tax.state.vt.us

JAY

Emeline Harmon
1036 VT RTE 242
Jay, VT   05859
802-988-2996
T-F 7-4
jay@tax.state.vt.us

JERICHO
Jessica R. Alexander
P.O. Box 67
Jericho, VT 05465
802-899-4936
M-Th 8-5; F 8-3;
and by appt.
jerichovermont@yahoo.com

JOHNSON
Rosemary Audibert
P.O. Box 383
Johnson, VT 05656
802-635-2611
M-F 7:30-4
raudibert@
townofjohnson.com

KILLINGTON
Judith J. Hansen
P.O. Box 429
Killington, VT 05751
802-422-3243
M-F 9-3
judy@town.killington.vt.us

KIRBY
Wanda L. Grant
346 Town Hall Road
Lyndonville, VT 05851
802-626-9386
T & Th 8-3
kirby@tax.state.vt.us

LANDGROVE
Casey Henson
P. O. Box 508
Londonderry, VT 05148
802-824-3716
Th 9-1 & by appt.
landgrove@tax.state.vt.us

LEICESTER
Donna F. Pidgeon
44 Schoolhouse Road
Leicester, VT 05733
802-247-5961
M T W 1-4

LEMINGTON
Norman Tallmage
2549 River Rd, VT 102
Lemington, VT 05903
802-277-4814
W 10-1
lemington@tax.state.vt.us

LINCOLN
Katherine Mikkelsen
62 Quaker Street
Lincoln, VT 05443
802-453-2980
T,W,Th,F 9-12 & 1-4; S 9-12
lnclnhillcntry@madriver.com

LONDONDERRY
James H. Twitchell
P.O. Box 118
S. Londonderry, VT 05155
802-824-3356
T-F 9-3; S 9-12
londonderry@tax.state.vt.us

LOWELL
Nanette Bonneau
2170 VT Rt. 100
Lowell, VT 05847
802-744-6559
M & Th 9-2:30
lowell@tax.state.vt.us

LUDLOW
Ulla P. Cook
P.O. Box 307
Ludlow, VT 05149
802-228-3232
M-F 8:30-4:30
treasure@ludlow.vt.us

LUNENBURG
Trudy Ann Parker
P.O. Box 54
Lunenburg, VT 05906
802-892-5959
M-Th 8:30-12 & 1-4;
F 8:30-12; Summer hours:
July-Sept. M-F 8:30-12

LYNDON
Lisa J. Barrett
P.O. Box 167
Lyndonville, VT 05851
802-626-5785
M-F 7:30-4:30
ltc@kingcon.com

MAIDSTONE
Susan Irwin
P.O. Box 118
Guildhall, VT 05905
802-676-3210
M & Th 9-11
maidstone@tax.state.vt.us

MANCHESTER
Linda L. Spence,
CMC/CVC
P.O. Box 830
Manchester Center, VT
05255
802-362-1315
M,T,Th,F 8:30-1 &
2-4:30;W 10-6
manclerk@sover.net

MARLBORO
Nora Wilson
P.O. Box E
Marlboro, VT 05344
802-254-2181
M,W,Th 9-4
marclerk@sover.net

MARSHFIELD

Bobbi Brimblecombe
122 School Street, Rm.1
Marshfield, VT 05658
802-426-3305
T-F 8:30-12 & 12:30-4:30
marshfield@innevi.com

MENDON

Ann Singiser
34 US Route 4
Mendon, VT 05701
802-775-1662
M,T,W 8-3; Th 8-1
mendonclerk@adelphia.net

MIDDLEBURY

Ann F. Webster
94 Main Street
Middlebury, VT 05753
802-388-8102
M-F 8:30-12 & 1-4:30
awebster@town.middle-
bury.vt.us

MIDDLESEX

June Lakin
5 Church Street
Middlesex, VT 05602
802-223-5915
M-Th 8-12 & 1-4:30
vermontjunebug@
yahoo.com

MIDDLETWN SPG

Laura Ann Castle
P. O. Box 1232
Middletown Springs, VT
05757
802-235-2220
M,T 9-12 & 1-4; F 1-4;
S 9-12

MILTON

John P. Cushing
P.O. Box 18
Milton, VT 05468
802-893-4111
M-F 8-5
jcushing@town.milton.vt.us

MONKTON

Carmelita C. Burritt
280 Monkton Ridge
N. Ferrisburgh, VT 05473
802-453-3800
M,T,Th,F 8-1; S 8:30-12

MONTGOMERY

Lynda Cluba
P.O. Box 356
Montgomery Center, VT
05471
802-326-4719
M T Th F 9-12 & 1-4;
W 9-12
montgomerytc@
surfglobal.net

MONTPELIER

Charlotte L. Hoyt
39 Main St.
Montpelier, VT 05602
802-223-9500
M-F 8-4:30
choyt@montpelier-vt.org

MORETOWN

Susan Goodyear
P.O. Box 666
Moretown, VT 05660
802-496-3645
M-Th 9-12 & 1-4:30;
F 9-3:30
moremuni@madriver.com

MORGAN

Tammylee Morin
P.O. Box 45
Morgan, VT 05853
802-895-2927
M 9-3; T & Th 8-3; W 8-5;
F 9-12

MORRISTOWN

Mary Ann Wilson
P. O. Box 748
Morrisville, VT 05661
802-888-6370
M,T,Th,F 8:30-4:30;
W 8:30-12:30
mawtclerk@pwshift.com

MT. HOLLY

Susan C. Covalla
P.O. Box 248
Mount Holly, VT 05758
802-259-2391
M-Th 8:30-4
mthollytc@vermontel.net

MT. TABOR

Ida R. Beauregard
P.O. Box 245
Mount Tabor, VT 05739
802-293-5282
T,W 9-12; and by appt.
mttabor@vermontel.net

NEW HAVEN

Barbara Torian
78 North Street
New Haven, VT 05472
802-453-3516
M-F 9-3

NEWARK

Joan Bicknell
1336 Newark Street
Newark, VT 05871
802-467-3336
M,W,Th 9-4

NEWBURY

Susan B. Underword
P.O. Box 126
Newbury, VT 05051
802-866-5521
M,W,Th,F 8:30-2:30;
T 8:30-6
newbury@sover.net

NEWFANE

Janice Litchfield
P.O. Box 36
Newfane, VT 05345
802-365-7772
M-F 9-3

NEWPORT CITY

James D. Johnson
222 Main Street
Newport, VT 05855
802-334-2112
M-F 8-4:30
cityclerk@newportver-
mont.org

NEWPORT TOWN

Denise Daigle
P. O. Box 85
Newport Center, VT 05857
802-334-6442
M-Th 7-4:30

NORTH HERO

Deborah D. Allen
P. O. Box 38
North Hero, VT 05474
802-372-6098
M-F 9-4; S 9-12

NORTHFIELD

Debra J. Russo
51 South Main Street
Northfield, VT 05663
802-485-5421
M-F 8-4:30
debrarusso@northfield.vt.us

NORTON

Miriam E. Nelson
P. O. Box 148
Norton, VT 05907
802-822-9935
M,T,Th 9-12 & 1:30-5;
F,S 9-12
norton@tax.state.vt.us

NORWICH

Bonnie J. Munday
P.O. Box 376
Norwich, VT 05055
802-649-1419
M-F 8:30-4:30; S 10-12
clerk@norwich.vt.us

ORANGE

Rita R. Bisson
P.O. Box 233
E. Barre, VT 05649
802-479-2673
M-F 8-12 & 1-4
biss256@aol.com

ORWELL

Susan Ann Arnebold
P.O. Box 32
Orwell, VT 05760
802-948-2032
M,T,Th,F 9:30-12 & 1-3:30
tckorwel@sover.net

PANTON

Susan F. Torrey
P.O. Box 174
Vergennes, VT 05491
802-475-2333
M,Th 9-5; T F 9-2; W 4-7
panton@gmavt.net

PAWLET

Joanne G. Waite
P.O. Box 128
Pawlet, VT 05761
802-325-3309
T,W,Th 9-3:30; F 9-12:30; &
by appt.
JWaite@vermontel.net

PEACHAM

Michael Bussiere
P.O. Box 244
Peacham, VT 05862
802-592-3218
T 9-1; W 4-7; Th 9-1 & 2-4;
F 9-1; S 9-1

PERU

Tracy Black
P.O. Box 127
Peru, VT 05152
802-824-3065
T,TH 8:30-4
perutown@sover.net

PITTSFIELD

Patricia S. Haskins
P.O. Box 556
Pittsfield, VT 05762
802-746-8170
T 12-6; W Th 9-3
pittsfield@tax.state.vt.us

PITTSFORD

Gordon R. Delong
P. O. Box 10
Pittsford, VT 05763
802-483-6500
M-F 8-4:30
pittsfrd@sover.net

PLAINFIELD

Linda Wells
P.O. Box 217
Plainfield, VT 05667
802-454-8461
M,W,F 7:30-4:00
plainfield@tax.state.vt.us

PLYMOUTH

Rachel Lynds
68 Town Office Rd.
Plymouth, VT 05056
802-672-3655
M-F 8:30-11:30 &
12:30-3:30
toplymouth@vermontel.net

POMFRET

Hazel B. Harrington
P.O. Box 286
N. Pomfret, VT 05053
802-457-3861
M,W,F 8-3

POULTNEY

Patricia A. McCoy,
CMC/AA
9 Main Street, Suite 2
Poultney, VT 05764
802-287-5761
M-F 8:30-12:30 & 1:30-4
poultney@vermontel.net

POWNAL

Karen J. Burrington
P.O. Box 411
Pownal, VT 05261
802-823-7757
M,W,Th,F 9-2; T 9-4
powclerk@sover.net

PROCTOR

Sidney Jones
45 Main Street
Proctor, VT 05765
802-459-3333
M-F 8-4

PUTNEY

Anita M. Coomes
P.O. Box 233
Putney, VT 05346
802-387-5862
M,W,Th,F 9-2; W 7-9pm;
S 9-12
anita1313@hotmail.com

RANDOLPH

Joyce L. Mazzucco,
CVC, CVT
Drawer B
Randolph, VT 05060
802-728-5682
M-F 8-12 & 1:00-4:30
clerk@municipaloffice.
randolph.vt.us

READING

Barbara J. Acuna
P.O. Box 72
Reading, VT 05062
802-484-7250
M-Th 9-4
reading@together.net

READSBORO

Deborah A. Calnan
P.O. Box 246
Readsboro, VT 05350
802-423-5405
M,T,Th,F 9-3
scooters@sover.net

RICHFORD

Gary A. Snider, CMC
P.O. Box 236
Richford, VT 05476
802-848-7751
M-F 8:30-4
richgas@together.net

RICHMOND

Velma E. Plouffe
P.O. Box 285
Richmond, VT 05477
802-434-2221
M 8-6; T-Th 8-4; F 8-1
vgodfrey@gmavt.net

RIPTON

Timothy Hanson
P.O. Box 10
Ripton, VT 05766
802-388-2266
M 2-6; T-F 9-1
ripton@tax.state.vt.us

ROCHESTER

Frances Guilmette
P.O. Box 238
Rochester, VT 05767
802-767-3631
T,W,Th,F 8-4; S 8-12
rochtown@sover.net

ROCKINGHAM

Doreen B. Aldrich
P.O. Box 339
Bellows Falls, VT 05101
802-463-4336
M-F 8:30-4:30
rbftnclk@sover.net

ROXBURY

Gloria B. Gerdes
P.O. Box 53
Roxbury, VT 05669
802-485-7840
T-F 9-12 & 1-4
townrox@nfld.tds.net

ROYALTON
Theresa M. Harrington
P.O. Box 680
S. Royalton, VT 05068
802-763-7207
T W Th 9-1 & 2-5
royalclerk@bluemoo.net

RUPERT
Andrea Lenhardt
P.O. Box 140
W. Rupert, VT 05776
802-394-7728
M 2-7; W 12-5; Th 10-3

RUTLAND CITY
Darlene A. Gregory
P.O. Box 969
Rutland, VT 05702
802-773-1801
M-F 8:30-5

RUTLAND TOWN
Annette Drinwater
P.O. Box 225
Center Rutland, VT 05736
802-773-2528
M-F 8-4:30
annette@rutlandtown.com

RYEGATE
Marsha Nelson
P. O. Box 332
Ryegate, VT 05042
802-584-3880
M,T,W 1-5; F 9-1
ryegate@tax.state.vt.us

SAINT ALBANS CITY
Dianna R. Baraby
P.O. Box 867
St. Albans, VT 05478
802-524-1501
M-F 7:30-4
staclerk@adelphia.net

SAINT ALBANS TOWN
Kathy S. Middlemiss
P.O. Box 37
St. Albans Bay, VT 05481
802-524-2415
M,T,Th,F 8-4
stalbtwn@adelphia.net

SAINT GEORGE
Shirley H. Vaux, CMCM
1 Barber Rd.
St. George, VT 05495
802-482-5272
M-F 8-12

SAINT JOHNSBURY
Sandra P. Grenier
1187 Main Street, Suite 2
St. Johnsbury, VT 05819
802-748-4331
M-F 8-5
stjaymanager@conriver.net

SALISBURY
June B. Hadley
P.O. Box 66
Salisbury, VT 05769
802-352-4228
T-F 9-3; 1st & 3rd S 9-12

SANDGATE

Ann B. Wuerslin
3266 Sandgate Road
Sandgate, VT 05250
802-375-9075
T & W 9-3;
Th a.m. by appt.
sanclerk@sover.net

SEARSBURG

Josephine Kilbride
P.O. Box 157
Wilmington, VT 05363
802-464-8081
M 8-4;T 8-12;F 8-12
josiekil@yahoo.com

SHAFTSBURY

Judith Stratton
P. O. Box 409
Shaftsbury, VT 05262
802-442-4038
M 9-5;T-F 9-2:30
Judy10@adelphia.net

SHARON

Joanne M. Slater
P.O. Box 250
Sharon, VT 05065
802-763-8268
M,T,Th 7:30-1 & 2-6;
W 7:30-12:30
town.of.sharon@valley.net

SHEFFIELD

Kathy Newland
P.O. Box 165
Sheffield, VT 05866
802-626-8862
M & F 8-2;W 8-2 & 5-8
sheffield@tax.state.vt.us

SHELBURNE

Colleen T. Haag
P.O. Box 88
Shelburne, VT 05482
802-985-5116
M-F 8:30-4:30
chaag@shelburnevt.org

SHELDON

Susan A. Burnor
P.O. Box 66
Sheldon, VT 05483
802-933-2524
M-F 8-3

SHOREHAM

Mary Jane James
297 Main Street
Shoreham, VT 05770
802-897-5841
M T W F 9-12 & 1-4
shoreham@tax.state.vt.us

SHREWSBURY
Anne Haley
9823 Cold River Road
Shrewsbury, VT 05738
802-492-3511
M-Th 10-3 & by appt.
shrewsbury@surfglobal.net

SOUTH BURLINGTON CITY
Donna Kinville
575 Dorset Street
S. Burlington, VT 05403
802-846-4105
M,T,Th,F 8-4:30; W 8-6:30
dkinville@sburl.com

SOUTH HERO
Sharon B. Roy
PO Box 175
South Hero, VT 05486
802-372-5552
M-Th 8:30-12 & 1-4:30

SPRINGFIELD
Bonnie L. Reynolds, CMC
96 Main Street
Springfield, VT 05156
802-885-2104
M-F 8-4:30
bonnie@vermontel.com

STAMFORD
Nancy L. Bushika
986 Main Road
Stamford, VT 05352
802-694-1361
T,W 11-4; Th 12-4 & 7-9;
F 12-4

STANNARD
Connie Withers
P.O. Box 94
Greensboro Bend, VT
05842
802-533-2577
W 8-12

STARKSBORO
Cheryl Estey
P.O. Box 91
Starksboro, VT 05487
802-453-2639
M,T,Th,F 9-5
starksboro@madriver.com

STOCKBRIDGE
Catherine Brown
P.O. Box 39
Stockbridge, VT 05772
802-234-9371
T,Th 9-3; W,F 9-12
dcbrown4@aol.com

STOWE

Alison Lewis
P.O. Box 248
Stowe, VT 05672
802-253-6133
M-F 7:30-4:30
townclerkoffice@townofs-
towevermont.org

STRAFFORD

Shelby A. Coburn
P.O. Box 27
Strafford, VT 05072
802-765-4421
T,W 8-5; Th 8-7; F 8-12
strafford@tax.state.vt.us

STRATTON

D. Kent Young
9 West Jamaica Road
Stratton, VT 05360
802-896-6184
M-Th 9-3
nottarts@sover.net

SUDBURY

Patricia Smith, CMC
4694 Rte. 30
Sudbury, VT 05733
802-623-7296
M 9-4; W,F 9-1
patsmith@sover.net

SUNDERLAND

Rose M. Keough
P.O. Box 295
E. Arlington, VT 05252
802-375-6106
M, T, Th 8-2; W 8-12 &
6-8; F by appt. only

SUTTON

Dorreen S. Devenger
P.O. Box 106
Sutton, VT 05867
802-467-3377
M,T,Th,F 9-5; W 9-12

SWANTON

Doris H. Raleigh
P.O. Box 711
Swanton, VT 05488
802-868-4421
M-F 8-4
swanton@adelphia.net

THETFORD

Roberta C. Howard
P.O. Box 126
Thetford Center, VT 05075
802-785-2922/4927
M 6-8 p.m.; T-F 8:30-3:30

TINMOUTH
Gail Fallar
515 North End Road
Tinmouth, VT 05773
802-446-2498
M & W 8-12 & 1-5
tinmouth@tax.state.vt.us

TOPSHAM
Juanita Claflin
P.O. Box 69
Topsham, VT 05076
802-439-5505
M 1-7; T Th F 9-4
topsham@tax.state.vt.us

TOWNSHEND
Cynthia A. Davis,
CVC/CMC
P.O. Box 223
Townshend, VT 05353
802-365-7300
M,T,W,F 9-4

TROY
Lucille Cadieux
P.O. Box 80
North Troy, VT 05859
802-988-2663
M-F 8-12 & 1-4
troy@tax.state.vt.us

TUNBRIDGE
Wendy McCullough
P.O. Box 6
Tunbridge, VT 05077
802-889-5521
M,T,Th,F 8-12 & 1-4;
W 9-6
towntun@innevi.com

UNDERHILL
Nancy C. Bradford
P.O. Box 32
Underhill Center, VT
05490
802-899-4434
M,T,Th,F 8-4 W 8-7
bradford@together.net

VERGENNES
Joan T. Devine, CVC/CVT
P.O. Box 35
Vergennes, VT 05491
802-877-2841
M-F 8-4:30
vergennes-
clerk@together.net

VERNON
Sandra B. Harris, CVC
567 Governor Hunt Road
Vernon, VT 05354
802-257-0292
M,T,W,F 8:30-4;
Th 8:30-6:30
vernontc@sover.net

VERSHIRE

Naomi LaBarr
6894 VT Rte 113
Vershire, VT 05079
802-685-2227
T-Th 8:30-3
vershire@tax.state.vt.us

VICTORY

Carol F. Easter
P.O. Box 609
N. Concord, VT 05858
802-328-2400
M 10-4; T-F by appt.;
S 10-1

WAITSFIELD

Sandra J. Gallup
9 Bridge Street
Waitsfield, VT 05673
802-496-2218
M-F 9-4
waitsfld@madriver.com

WALDEN

Lina Smith
12 VT RTE 215
W. Danville, VT 05873
802-563-2220
M,T,F 9-3:30; Th 9-5
waldentc@sover.net

WALLINGFORD

Joyce Barbieri
P. O. Box 327
Wallingford, VT 05773
802-446-2336
M-Th 8-4:30 F 8-12
townclerk@
wallingfordvt.com

WALTHAM

Mary Kinson
P. O. Box 175
Vergennes, VT 05491
802-877-3641
T & F 9-3
waltham@tax.state.vt.us

WARDSBORO

Jacqueline E. Bedard
P.O. Box 48
Wardsboro, VT 05355
802-896-6055
M-Th 9-12 & 1-4:30

WARREN

Reta K. Goss
P.O. Box 337
Warren, VT 05674
802-496-2709
M-F 9-4:30
warrenvttc@hotmail.com

WASHINGTON

Carol Davis
2895 VT Rt. 110
Washington, VT 05675
802-883-2218
M & T 8:30-2:30
washington@tax.state.vt.us

WATERBURY

Donna Centonze
51 South Main Street
Waterbury, VT 05676
802-244-8447
M-F 8-4:30
dcxi@aol.com

WATERFORD

Joanne Jurentkuff
P.O. Box 56
Lower Waterford, VT
05848
802-748-2122
M,Th,F 8:30-3:30; T 12-6
waterford@tax.state.vt.us

WATERVILLE

Nancy LaRose
P.O. Box 31
Waterville, VT 05492
802-644-8865
M,T,Th 9-1:30
waterville@tax.state.vt.us

WEATHERSFIELD

Flo-Ann Dango
P. O. Box 550
Ascutney, VT 05030
802-674-2626
M-W 9-4; Th 9-5
tclerk@weathersfield.org

WELLS

Katharine R. Bergen
P.O. Box 585
Wells, VT 05774
802-645-0486
M-F 9-3 and by appt.
krbergen@earthlink.net

WEST FAIRLEE

Nancy M. Bragg
P.O. Box 615
W. Fairlee, VT 05083
802-333-9696
M,W,F 10-4

WEST HAVEN

Carol L. Richards
2919 Main Road
West Haven, VT 05743
802-265-4880
M & W 1-3:30
westhaven@tax.state.vt.us

WEST RUTLAND

Jayne L. Pratt, CVC
35 Marble Street
W. Rutland, VT 05777
802-438-2204
M-Th 9-12 & 1-4; F by appt.
jprattwrutland@aol.com

WEST WINDSOR

Cathy B. Archibald
P.O. Box 6
Brownsville, VT 05037
802-484-7212
M-F 9-12 & 1:30-4:30

WESTFIELD

Connie La Plume
1257 VT Rt. 100
Westfield, VT 05874
802-744-2484
M 8-5; T 10-5; W 8-5
westfield@tax.state.vt.us

WESTFORD

Nanette Rogers
1713 Vt. Route 128
Westford, VT 05494
802-878-4587
M-F 8:30-4:30
westfdvt@together.net

WESTMINSTER

Penny L. Muzzey
P.O. Box 147
Westminster, VT 05158
802-722-4091
M-F 8:30-4
westmntc@sover.net

WESTMORE

Diane M. Parenteau
54 Hinton Hill Road
Orleans, VT 05860
802-525-3007
M-Th 9-12 & 1-4
memerep@surfglobal.net

WESTON

Sandra M. Goodwin
P.O. Box 98
Weston, VT 05161
802-824-6645
M-F 9-1
Weston99@sover.net

WEYBRIDGE

Karen B. Curavoo
1727 Quaker Village Road
Weybridge, VT 05753
802-545-2450
M T Th F 9-2
weybrdge@together.net

WHEELOCK

Michelle Trottier
P.O. Box 1328
Lyndonville, VT 05851
802-626-9094
T & W 8:30-3 Th 1-8

WHITING

Grace E. Simonds
29 South Main Street
Whiting, VT 05778
802-623-7813
M W 9-12 & 4-6; F 9-12;
and by appt.
whiting@tax.state.vt.us

WHITINGHAM

Earle S. Holland, Jr.
P.O. Box 529
Jacksonville, VT 05342
802-368-7887
M-F 9-2; W 5:30-7:30;
1st Sat. 9-2
whitingham@tax.state.vt.us

WILLIAMSTOWN

Deborah Palmer
P.O. Box 646
Williamstown, VT 05679
802-433-5455
T-F 8-12 & 12:30-4:30
clerk@sover.net

WILLISTON

Deborah Beckett
7900 Williston Road
Williston, VT 05495
802-878-5121
M 8-6; T-F 8-4:30
beckettd@
willistontown.com

WILMINGTON

Susan Manton
P.O. Box 217
Wilmington, VT 05363
802-464-5836
M-W 8:30-12 & 1-4;
Th 8:30-4; F 8:30-6:30
wilmclrk@together.net

WINDHAM

Carol C. Merritt
5976 Windham Hill Rd
Windham, VT 05359
802-874-4211
T,Th,F 10-3; and by appt.

WINDSOR

Sandra Hinkley Jarvis
PO Box 47
Windsor, VT 05089
802-674-5610
M,W,Th 8-4:30; T 8-6;
F 8-2

WINHALL

Marion Jenks
P.O. Box 389
Bondville, VT 05340
802-297-2122
M-Th 9-12

WINOOSKI

Pauline K. Schmoll, CMC,
CVT, CVC
27 West Allen Street
Winooski, VT 05404
802-655-6419
M-F 8-4
pkschmoll@onioncity.com

WOLCOTT

Linda J. Martin
P.O. Box 100
Wolcott, VT 05680
802-888-2746
T-F 8-4 Tues. eve. 6-8
wolcott@pshift.com

WOODBURY

Marcia McGlynn
P.O. Box 10
Woodbury, VT 05681
802-456-7051
T-Th 8:30-1; Thurs. eve. 6-8
towoodbury@aol.com

WOODFORD

Aileen O'Neil,
CMC/AAE/CVC
1391 VT RTE 9
Woodford, VT 05201
802-442-4895
M-Th 8:30-12 & by appt.
woodford@tax.state.vt.us

WOODSTOCK

Jerome R. (Jay) Morgan
31 The Green
Woodstock, VT 05091
802-457-3611
M-F 8-12 & 1-4:30
jay@townofwoodstock.org

WORCESTER

Carolyn (Lindy) Wells,
CVC, CVT
Drawer 161
Worcester, VT 05682
802-223-6942
M,T,Th 8-4 (closed 12-1
when necessary); F 8-1
worster@madriver.com

–Appendix C–
CALIFORNIA DOMESTIC PARTNERSHIP LAW

FAMILY.CODE SECTION 297

297. (a) Domestic partners are two adults who have chosen to share one another's lives in an intimate and committed relationship of mutual caring.

(b) A domestic partnership shall be established in California when all of the following requirements are met:

(1) Both persons have a common residence.

(2) Both persons agree to be jointly responsible for each other's basic living expenses incurred during the domestic partnership.

(3) Neither person is married or a member of another domestic partnership.

(4) The two persons are not related by blood in a way that would prevent them from being married to each other in this state.

(5) Both persons are at least 18 years of age.

(6) Either of the following:

(A) Both persons are members of the same sex.

(B) One or both of the persons meet the eligibility criteria under Title II of the Social Security Act as defined in 42 U.S.C. Section 402(a) for old-age insurance benefits or Title XVI of the Social Security Act as defined in 42 U.S.C. Section 1381 for aged individuals. Notwithstanding any other provision of this section, persons of opposite sexes may not constitute a domestic partnership unless one or both of the persons are over the age of 62.

(7) Both persons are capable of consenting to the domestic partnership.

(8) Neither person has previously filed a Declaration of Domestic Partnership with the Secretary of State pursuant to this division that has not been terminated under Section 299.

(9) Both file a Declaration of Domestic Partnership with the Secretary of State pursuant to this division.

(c) "Have a common residence" means that both domestic partners share the same residence. It is not necessary that the legal right to possess the common residence be in both of their names. Two people have a common residence even if one or both have additional residences. Domestic partners do not cease to have a common residence if one leaves the common residence but intends to return.

(d) "Basic living expenses" means shelter, utilities, and all other costs directly related to the maintenance of the common household of the common residence of the domestic partners. It also means any other cost, such as medical care, if some or all of the cost is paid as a benefit because a person is another person's domestic partner.

(e) "Joint responsibility" means that each partner agrees to provide for the other partner's basic living expenses if the partner is unable to provide for herself or himself. Persons to whom these expenses are owed may enforce this responsibility if, in extending credit or providing goods or services, they relied on the existence of the domestic partnership and the agreement of both partners to be jointly responsible for those specific expenses.

FAMILY.CODE SECTION 299

299. (a) A domestic partnership is terminated when any one of the following occurs:

(1) One partner gives or sends to the other partner a written notice by certified mail that he or she is terminating the partnership.

(2) One of the domestic partners dies.

(3) One of the domestic partners marries.

(4) The domestic partners no longer have a common residence.

(b) Upon termination of a domestic partnership, at least one former partner shall file a Notice of Termination of Domestic Partnership with the Secretary of State by mailing a completed form to the Secretary of State by certified mail. The date on which the Notice of Termination of Domestic Partnership is received by the Secretary of State shall be deemed the actual termination date of the domestic partnership, unless termination is caused by the death or marriage of a domestic partner, in which case the actual termination date shall be the date indicated on the Notice of Termination of Domestic Partnership form. The partner who files the Notice of Termination of Domestic Partnership shall send a copy of the notice to the last known address of the other partner.

(c) A former domestic partner who has given a copy of a Declaration of Domestic Partnership to any third party in order to qualify for any benefit or right shall, within 60 days of termination of the domestic partnership, give or send to the third party, at the last known address of the third party, written notification that the domestic partnership has been terminated. A third party who suffers a loss as a result of failure by the domestic partner to send this notice shall be entitled to seek recovery from the partner who was obligated to send it for any actual loss resulting thereby.

(d) Failure to provide the third-party notice required in subdivision (c) shall not delay or prevent the termination of the domestic partnership.

–Appendix D–
STATE DEPARTMENTS OF VITAL RECORDS

Contact your local office for birth certificate changes.

ALABAMA

Vital Records
State Department of
Public Health
P.O. Box 5625
Montgomery, AL
36103-5625
334-206-5418
www.adph.org

ALASKA

Bureau of Vital Statistics
Department of Health and
Social Services
P.O. Box 110675
Juneau, AK 99811-0675
907-465-3391
www.hss.state.ak.us

AMERICAN SAMOA

Registrar of Vital Statistics
Vital Statistics Section
Government of American
Samoa
Pago Pago, AS 96799
684-633-1222, ext. 214

ARIZONA

Office of Vital Records
Arizona Department of
Health Services
P.O. Box 3887
Phoenix, AZ 85030-3887
602-364-1300
www.hs.state.az.us

ARKANSAS
Division of Vital Records
Arkansas Department of
Health
Slot #44
4815 West Markham Street
Little Rock, AR 72201
501-661-2336
www.healthyarkansas.com.

CALIFORNIA
Office of Vital Records
Department of Health
Services
304 "S" Street
P.O. Box 730241
Sacramento, CA
94244-0241
916-445-2684
www.dhs.ca.gov/hisp/chs/ov
r/ordercert.htm

CANAL ZONE
Correspondence Branch
Passport Services
U.S. Department of State
1111 19th Street NW,
Suite 510
Washington, DC
20522-1705
202-955-0307

COLORADO
Vital Records
Colorado Department of
Public Health and
Environment
4300 Cherry Creek Dr., S
HSVRD-VS-A1
Denver, CO 80246-1530
303-756-4464
www.cdphe.state.co.us
/hs/certs.asp

CONNECTICUT
Department of Public
Records
Vital Records Section
410 Capitol Avenue
PO Box 340308
MS#11VRS
Hartford, CT 06134-0308
860-509-7896
www.dph.state.ct.us/OPPE
/hpvital.htm

DELAWARE
Office of Vital Statistics
Division of Public Health
P.O. Box 637
Dover, DE 19903
302-744-4549

DISTRICT OF COLUMBIA
Vital Records Office
825 North Capitol St. NE
lst Floor
Washington, DC 20002
202-442-9009
www.dchealth.dc.gov.

FLORIDA
Office of Vital Statistics
P.O. Box 210
1217 Pearl Street
Jacksonville, FL 32231
904-359-6900
www.doh.state.fl.us.

GEORGIA
Vital Records
2600 Skyland Drive, NE
Atlanta, GA 30319-3640
404-679-4701
www.state.ga.us/programs
/vitalrecords

GUAM
Office of Vital Statistics
Department of Public
Health and Social Services
Government of Guam
P.O. Box 2816
Agana, GU, M.I. 96910
671-734-4589.

HAWAII
State Department of Health
Office of Health Status
Monitoring
Vital Records Section
P.O. Box 3378
Honolulu, HI 96801
808-586-4533
www.state.hi.us/doh/records
/vital_records.html

IDAHO
Vital Statistics
450 West State Street,
1st Floor
P.O. Box 83720
Boise, ID 83720-0036
208-334-5988
www.state.id.us/dhw

ILLINOIS
Division of Vital Records
Illinois Department of
Public Health
605 West Jefferson Street
Springfield, IL 62702-5097
217-782-6553
www.idph.state.il.us

INDIANA
Vital Records Section
State Department of Health
2 North Meridian Street
Indianapolis, IN 46204
317-233-2700
www.in.gov/isdh/index.htm

IOWA

Iowa Department of
Public Health
Bureau of Vital Records
Lucas Office Building,
1st Floor
321 East 12th Street
Des Moines, IA 50319-0075
515-281-4944
www.idph.state.ia.us/pa
/vr.htm

KANSAS

Office of Vital Statistics
1000 SW Jackson St.,
Suite 120
Topeka, Kansas 66612-2221
785-296-1400
www.kdhe.state.ks.us/vital/

KENTUCKY

Office of Vital Statistics
Department for Health
Services
275 East Main Street
Frankfort, KY 40621-0001
502-564-4212
http://publichealth.
   state.ky.us/vital.htm

LOUISIANA

Vital Records Registry
Office of Public Health
325 Loyola Avenue
New Orleans, LA 70112
504-568-5152
www.dhh.state.la.us

MAINE

Office of Vital Records
Maine Department of
Human Resources
221 State Street
11 State House Station
Augusta, ME 04333-0011
207-287-3181
www.state.me.us

MARYLAND

Division of Vital Records
Department of Health and
Mental Hygiene
6550 Reisterstown Road
P.O. Box 68760
Baltimore, MD 21215-0020
410-764-3038
http://mdpublichealth.org
/vsa

MASSACHUSETTS

Registry of Vital Records
and Statistics
150 Mount Vernon Street,
1st Floor
Dorchester, MA
02125-3105
617-740-2600
www.state.ma.us/dph
/bhsre/rvr/vrcopies.htm

MICHIGAN

Vital Records
3423 North Martin Luther
King Blvd.
P.O. Box 30195
Lansing, MI 48909
517-335-8656
www.mdch.state.mi.us
/pha/osr

MINNESOTA

Minnesota Department of
Health
Section of Vital Statistics
717 Delaware Street, SE
P.O. Box 9441
Minneapolis, MN 55440
612-676-5120
www.health.state.mn.us

MISSISSIPPI

Mississippi Vital Records
State Department of Health
2423 North State Street
Jackson, MS 39216
601-576-7981/
601-576-7450
www.ms.gov

MISSOURI

Missouri Department of
Health
Bureau of Vital Records
930 Wildwood
P.O. Box 570
Jefferson City, MO
65102-0570
573-751-6400
www.health.state.mo.us
/birthanddeathrecords

MONTANA

Dept of Public Health and
Human Services
Vital Records
P.O. Box 4210
Helena, MT 59604
406-444-4228
www.dphhs.mt.gov

NEBRASKA

Vital Records
Department of Health and
Human Services
301 Centennial Mall South
P.O. Box 95065
Lincoln, NE 68509-5065
402-471-2871
www.hhs.state.ne.us/ced
/nevrinfo.htm

NEVADA

Office of Vital Records
Capitol Complex
505 East King Street #102
Carson City, NV 89710
775-684-4280
http://health2k.state.nv.us

NEW HAMPSHIRE

Bureau of Vital Records
6 Hazen Drive
Concord, NH 03301
603-271-4654
www.dhhs.state.nh.us

NEW JERSEY

New Jersey State
Department of Health and
Senior Services
Vital Statistics Registration
P.O. Box 370
Trenton, NJ 08625-0370
609-292-4087
www.state.nj.us/health
/vital/vital.htm.

NEW MEXICO

Vital Records
New Mexico Health
Services Division
P.O. Box 26110
Santa Fe, NM 87502
505-827-2338

NEW YORK

(except New York City)
Birth or Death Unit
Vital Records Section
P.O. Box 2602
Albany, NY 12220-2602
518-474-3075
www.health.state.ny.state

NEW YORK CITY

Office of Vital Records
NYC Department of Health
125 Worth St., CN4,
Rm. 133
New York, NY 10013
212-788-4520
www.nyc.gov/health

NORTH CAROLINA

NC Vital Records
1903 Mail Service Center
Raleigh, NC 27699-1903
919-733-3526
www.schs.state.nc.us/SCHS/

NORTH DAKOTA

Division of Vital Records
State Capitol
600 East Boulevard Avenue
Bismarck, ND 58505-0200
701-328-2360
www.health.state.nd.us

NORTHERN MARIANA

Islands
Superior Court
Vital Records Section
P.O. Box 307
Saipan, MP 96950
670-234-6401, ext. 15

OHIO

Bureau of Vital Statistics
Ohio Department of Health
P.O. Box 15098
Columbus, OH 43216-0118
614-466-2531
www.odh.state.oh.us/birth
/birthmain.htm

OKLAHOMA

Vital Records Service
State Department of Health
1000 Northeast 10th Street
Oklahoma City, OK 73117
405-271-4040
www.health.state.ok.us
/program/vital/brec/html

OREGON

Oregon Health Division
Vital Records
P.O. Box 14050
Portland, OR 97293-0050
503-731-4095.
www.ohd.hr.state.or.us

PENNSYLVANIA

Division of Vital Records
101 South Mercer Street
Room 401
P.O. Box 1528
New Castle, PA 16101
724-656-3100
http://webserver.health.
state.pa.us/health/site

PUERTO RICO

Department of Health
Demographic Registry
P.O. Box 11854
Fernández Juncos Station
San Juan, PR 00910
787-728-7980

RHODE ISLAND

Division of Vital Records
Rhode Island Department
of Health
3 Capitol Hill, Room 101
Providence, RI 02908-5097
401-222-2811

SOUTH CAROLINA

Office of Vital Records
SC DHEC
2600 Bull Street
Columbia, SC 29201
803-898-3630
www.myscgov.com

SOUTH DAKOTA

Vital Records
State Department of Health
600 East Capitol Avenue
Pierre, SD 57501-2536
605-773-4961
www.state.sd.us/doh
/vitalrec/vital.htm

TENNESSEE

Tennessee Vital Records
Central Services Building
421 5th Avenue, North
Nashville, TN 37247
615-741-1763
www.state.tn.us/health/vr
/index.htm

TEXAS

Bureau of Vital Statistics
Texas Department of
Health
P.O. Box 12040
Austin, TX 78711-2040
512-458-7111
www.tdh.state.tx.us/bvs

UTAH

Office of Vital Records
Utah Department of Health
288 North 1460 West
P.O. Box 141012
Salt Lake City, UT
84114-1012
801-538-6105
http://hlunix.hl.state.ut
.us/bvr

VERMONT

Vermont
Department of Health
Vital Records Section
P. O. Box 70
108 Cherry Street
Burlington, VT 05402
802-863-7275

(Records prior to the
latest 10 years.)
Public Records
Reference and Research
US Route 2—Middlesex
Drawer 33
Montpelier, VT 05633-7601
802-828-3286

VIRGINIA

Office of Vital Records
P.O. Box 1000
Richmond, VA 23218-1000
804-662-6200
www.vdh.state.va.us

WASHINGTON

Department of Health
Center for Health Statistics
P.O. Box 9709
Olympia, WA 98507-9709
360-236-4300
www.doh.wa.gov

WEST VIRGINIA

Vital Registration Office
Room 165
350 Capitol Street
Charleston, WV
25301-3701
304-558-2931
www.wvdhhr.org

WISCONSIN

Vital Records
1 West Wilson Street
P.O. Box 309
Madison, WI 53701
608-266-1371
www.dhfs.state.wi.us
  /vitalrecords

WYOMING

Vital Records Services
Hathaway Building
Cheyenne, WY 82002
307-777-7591
http://wdhfs.state.wy.us

–Appendix E–
RESOURCES

MAGAZINES

The Advocate
P.O. Box 4371
Los Angeles, CA 90078
815-734-1157
www.advocate.com

Alternative Family Magazine
www.altfammag.com

And Baby magazine
www.andbabymag.com

Curve Magazine
1550 Bryant Street
Suite 510
San Francisco, CA 94103
800-705-0070
www.curvemag.com

Gay Parents Magazine
P.O. Box 750852,
Forest Hills, NY 11375-0852
718-997-0392
www.gayparentmag.com

Girlfriends
  415-648-9464
  www.gfriends.com

Lesbian News
  800-458-9888
  www.lesbiannews.com

Our World (gay travel)
  Our World Publishing Corp.
  1104 North Nova Road, Suite 251
  Daytona Beach, FL 32117, USA
  386-441-5367
  www.ourworldpublishing.com

Out Magazine
  6922 Hollywood Blvd, 10th Floor
  Los Angeles, CA 90028
  815-734-1157
  www.out.com

Whosoever (gay Christian magazine)
  Whosoever Ministries, Inc.
  P.O. Box 160177
  Atlanta, GA 30316
  www.iwgonline.org

BOOKS

BOOKS FOR ADULTS

4 Steps to Financial Security for Lesbian and Gay Couples
  by Harold L. Lustig

Bisexual Resource Guide: Expanded
  by Robyn Ochs

Ceremonies of the Heart: Celebrating Lesbian Unions
by Becky Butler

Choosing Assisted Reproduction: Social, Emotional & Ethical Considerations
by Susan Cooper, Ellen Sarasohn Glazer

Coming Out to Parents: A Two-Way Survival Guide for Lesbians and Gay Men and Their Parents
by Mary V. Borhek

Equal Rites: Lesbian and Gay Worship, Ceremonies, and Celebrations
by Kittredge Cherry

The Essential Guide to Lesbian and Gay Weddings
by Tess Ayers, Paul Brown

Fatherhood for Gay Men: An Emotional and Practical Guide to Becoming a Gay Dad
by Kevin McGarry

Gay Widowers: Life After the Death of a Partner
by Michael Shernoff

A Grief Recovery Guide for Gay Men
by David Wayne Silva

How to Make the World a Better Place for Gays and Lesbians
by Una W. Fahy

How to Write Your Own Living Will
by Edward A. Haman

The Ins and Outs of Gay Sex: A Medical Handbook for Men
by Stephen E. Goldstone

*J.K. Lasser's Gay Finances in a Straight World: A Comprehensive
Financial Planning Handbook*
  by Peter M. Berkery

*The Lesbian and Gay Parenting Handbook: Creating and Raising
Our Families*
  by April Martin

Living Trusts and Other Ways to Avoid Probate
  by Karen Ann Rolcik

A Matter of Trust: The Guide to Gestational Surrogacy
  by Gail Dutton

*Men Like Us : The GMHC Complete Guide to Gay Men's Sexual,
Physical, and Emotional Well-Being*
  by Daniel Wolfe

*My Gender Workbook: How to Become a Real Man, a Real
Woman, the Real You, or Something Else Entirely*
  by Kate Bornstein

My Guy
  by Martin Kantor, M.D.

*Now That You Know: What Every Parent Should Know About
Homosexuality*
  by Betty Fairchild

*Out & About Campus: Personal Accounts by Lesbian, Gay,
Bisexual & Transgender College Students*
  by Kim Howard

*Outing Yourself: How to Come Out as Lesbian or Gay to Your
Family, Friends, and Coworkers*
  by Michelangelo Signorile

Power of Attorney Handbook
by Edward A. Haman

Practical Tools for Foster Parents
by Lana Temple-Plotz

The Queer Parent's Primer: A Lesbian and Gay Families' Guide to Navigating Through a Straight World
by Stephanie A. Brill

The Rights of People Who are HIV Positive
by William B. Rubenstein, et al

Try This at Home! A Do-It-Yourself Guide for Instituting Lesbian/Gay Rights Policy.
by Matthew A. Coles

The Ultimate Guide to Pregnancy for Lesbians: Tips and Techniques from Conception to Birth: How to Stay Sane and Care for Yourself
by Rachel Pepper

Unmarried Parents' Rights
by Jacqueline D. Stanley

U.S. Immigration Step by Step
by Edwin T. Gania

The Visitation Handbook: Your Complete Guide to Parenting Apart
by Brette McWhorter Sember

When It's Time to Leave Your Lover: A Guide For Gay Men
by Neil Kaminsky

BOOKS FOR CHILDREN

ABC A Family Alphabet Book
   by Bobbie Combs

All Families Are Different
   by Sol Gordon

Coping When a Parent Is Gay (Coping)
   by Deborah A. Miller

Daddy's Roommate
   by Michael Willhoite

Heather Has Two Mommies
   by Leslea Newman

Two Moms, the Zark, and Me
   by Johnny Valentine

When Grown-Ups Fall in Love
   by Barbara Lynn Edmonds

Zack's Story: Growing Up With Same-Sex Parents
   by Keith Elliot Greenberg

HOTLINES FOR DOMESTIC VIOLENCE

National Coalition Against Domestic Violence (can provide state
and local numbers for domestic violence assistance)
www.ncadv.org/resources/state.htm 1-800-799-SAFE (7233).

National Domestic Violence Hotline
www.ndvh.org/
800-799-7233

ORGANIZATIONS

AIDS

AIDS Memorial Quilt Project
PO Box 5552
Atlanta, GA 31107
404-688-5500
www.aidsquilt.org

American Academy of HIV Medicine
836 N. La Cienega Blvd., Suite 303
Los Angeles, CA 90069-4708
310-278-6380
www.aahivm.org

The Center for AIDS
Hope and Remembrance Project
P.O. Box 66306, Houston, TX 77266-6306
1407 Hawthorne, Houston, TX 77006
Toll Free: 888-341-1788
www.centerforaids.org

HOSPICE CARE

The National Hospice and Palliative Care Organization
1700 Diagonal Road, Suite 625
Alexandria, VA 22314
703-37-1500
www.nhpo.org

LEGAL

American Bar Association AIDS Coordination Project
740 15th Street, N.W.
Washington, DC 20005-1019

202-662-1028

The Center for Lesbian and Gay Civil Rights
1211 Chestnut Street, Suite 605
Philadelphia, PA 19107
215-731-1447
www.center4civilrights.org

GLAD Gay and Lesbian Advocates and Defenders
294 Washington Street, Suite 301
Boston, MA 02108
617-426-1350
www.glad.org

Human Rights Campaign (HRC)
919 18th St., N.W., Suite 800
Washington, D.C. 20006
202-628-4160
www.hrc.org

Lambda Legal
120 Wall Street, Suite 1500
New York, NY 10005-3904
212-809-8585 phone
212-809-0055 fax
www.lambdalegal.org

Service Members Legal Defense Network
PO Box 65301
Washington DC 20035-5301
202-328-FAIR
www.sldn.org/templates/index.html

Vermont Bar Association
800-639-7036
www.vtbar.org

MEDICAL

Gay and Lesbian Medical Association
459 Fulton Street
Suite 107
San Francisco, CA 94102
Physician referral: 877-LGBTDOC
Reimbursement help line: 888-VACCRIX

RELIGIOUS

Dignity/USA
1500 Massachusetts Avenue, NW
Suite 11 Y
Washington, D.C. 20005
800-877-8797
www.dignityusa.org

Jewish Advocacy for Gays, Lesbians, Bisexuals and Transgenders
585-586-3105

SUPPORT

National Association of Lesbian, Gay, Bisexual, and Transgender
Community Centers (NALGBTCC) – directory of local centers
12832 Garden Grove Blvd., Suite A
Garden Grove, CA 92843
www.lgbtcenters.org

TRANSGENDER (TG)

International Foundation for Gender Education
P.O. Box 540229
Waltham, MA 02454-0229
781-899-2212
www.ifge.org

ONLINE INFORMATION AND DOCUMENTS

ACTIVISM, RIGHTS AND GENERAL INFORMATION AND SUPPORT

www.equalityproject.org (Gay Shareholder Activism)
www.gay.com
http://gaywork.com
www.lesbian.org
www.nclrights.org (lesbian rights)
www.pridelinks.com
www.pridenet.com
www.queeramerica.com
www.rainbowquery.com

ADOPTION

Gay Adoption Mailing List
http://maelstrom.stjohns.edu/archives/gay-aparent.html

Gay and lesbian adoptions
www.adoptions.com/gaylez.html

State by state GLBT gay friendly adoption agencies
www.hrc.org/familynet/adoption_groups.asp

State gay adoption laws
www.lambdalegal.org/cgi-bin/iowa/documents
/record?record=399

AIDS

The Body: An AIDS and HIV Information Resource
www.thebody.com

BISEXUAL

BiNet
www.binetusa.org

Bisexual
www.bi.org

Bisexual Aware Professionals
www.bizone.org/bap

Bisexual Foundation
www.bisexual.org

Bisexual Resource Center
www.biresource.org

CALIFORNIA DOMESTIC PARTNERSHIPS

CA declaration of domestic partnership
www.ss.ca.gov/business/sf/forms/sf-dp1.pdf

CA termination of domestic partnership
www.ss.ca.gov/business/sf/forms/sf-dpterm.pdf

CHILDREN OF GAY PARENTS

Children of Lesbians and Gays
www.colage.org

Family Pride Coalition
http://familypride.org

DIVORCE

The Gay Divorcee Research Project
www.gldivorce.net

DOMESTIC PARTNERSHIPS

ACLU list of states and states recognizing domestic partnerships,
also list of employers offering benefits
www.aclu.org

Churches/denominations that support gay ceremonies
www.buddybuddy.com/toc.html

Newspapers that print commitment ceremony announcements
www.glaad.org

Sample domestic partnership agreements:
www.hrc.org/familynet/documents/4c75a104.pdf
www.buddybuddy.com/d-p-simp.html
www.buddybuddy.com/d-p-samp.html

DOMESTIC VIOLENCE

The Network
www.thenetworklared.org

www.rainbowdomesticviolence.itgo.com

EDUCATION

See Schools

EMPLOYMENT

Corporate Index
www.hrc.org/worknet/cei/cei_report.pdf

FINANCES

Gay Financial Network
www.gfn.com

www.domparts.com

FOSTER PARENTING

www.fosterparenting.com

National Foster Parent Association
www.nfpainc.org

FRATERNITIES AND SORORITIES

Lambda 10
www.lambda10.org

GLBT fraternities and sororities
www.bglad.com/education_and_learning/fraternities_and
_sororities

HEALTH CARE DIRECTIVES

http://public.findlaw.com/healthcare/forms.html

HETEROSEXUAL MARRIAGE

Gamma
www.gaymarriedmen.org (support for gay married men)

HIV

AEGIS (comprehensive HIV information center)
www.aegis.com

HIV In Site
http://hivinsite.ucsf.edu

HIV Positive.com
www.hivpositive.com

American Medical Association
www.ama-assn.org

The Body: An AIDS and HIV Information Resource
www.thebody.com

GRIEF

Lesbians and Gays End of Life Issues
www.growthhouse.org/gayissue.html

IMMIGRATION

Lesbian and Gay Immigration Rights Task Force
www.lgirtf.org/ 212-714-2904

Queer Immigration
www.qrd.org/qrd/www/world/immigration/index.html

INSEMINATION

www.gayhealthchannel.com/AI/

INSURANCE

List of insurers offering gay friendly policies
www.buddybuddy.com/d-p-ins.html

INTERNATIONAL ORGANIZATIONS

The International Lesbian and Gay Association
www.ilga.org

LIFE INSURANCE

HIV and insurance
www.HIVpositive.com

Medical Information Bureau
www.mib.com

MEDICAL

AIDS Information Global Education System
www.aidsinfo.org

Association of Gay and Lesbian Psychiatrists Referral Service
215-222-2800
www.aglp.org

Gay and Lesbian Medical Association
www.glma.org

www.gayhealth.com

Gay Men's Health Crisis
www.gmhc.org

www.gayhealthchannel.com

Lesbian Community Cancer Project
773-561-4662
www.lccp.org

Lesbian STD
http://dpts.washington.edu/wswstd

www.lesbianhealth.net

Mary-Helen Mautner Project for Lesbians with Cancer
202-332-5536
www.mautnerproject.org

National Association on HIV over 50
816-421-5263
www.hivoverfifty.org

www.safersex.org

MILITARY

Center for the Study of Sexual Minorities in the Military
www.gaymilitary.ucsb.edu

ORGAN DONATION

www.organdonor.gov

PARENTING

www.familieslikeours.org
www.familypride.org
www.gayfamilyoptions.org
www.geocities.com/gayparenting
www.haydennet.com/parenting
www.lesbian.org/lesbian-moms/index.html
www.ourfamily.org
www.proudparenting.com
www.queerparents.org

PHYSICIAN ASSISTED SUICIDE

www.finalexit.org

PRIDE EVENTS

www.interpride.org

REAL ESTATE

Gay and Lesbian Realtor Referral and Relocation Network
http://homelounge.com

RELIGION

DignityUSA: GLBT Catholics
www.dignityusa.org

Interfaith Working Group Online
www.iwgonline.org

Second Stone list of lesbian/gay/bisexual/transsexual-friendly
Christian churches:
www.qrd.org/QRD/religion

RETIREMENT

Gay Retirement
www.gayretirement.org

Lesbian and Gay Aging Issues Network
www.asaging.org/lgain

National Gay and Lesbian Task Force Aging Initiative
www.ngltf.org

SCHOOLS

Campus Pride
www.campuspride.net

Colleges and Universities with anti-discrimination policies
http://www.hrc.org

Colleges and Universities with programs in gay and lesbian studies
http://www.queertheory.com/academics/schools

Gay-Lesbian Straight Education Network
www.glsen.org

National Consortium of Directors of LGTB Resources in
Higher Education
www.lgbtcampus.org

Office of Civil Rights, US Department of Education
www.ed.gov/offices/OCR

SENIORS

Gay Friendly Senior Housing
www.hrc.org/familynet/documents/3c62b.pdf

Lesbian and Gay Aging issues Network
http://www.asaging.org/lgain

Pride Senior Network
212-271-7288
www.pridesenior.org

Senior Action in a Gay Environment (SAGE)
212-741-2247
www.sageusa.org

Transgender (TG) Aging Network
www.forge-forward.org/TAN

STDS

CDC National Center for HIV, STD and TB Prevention
http://www.cdc.gov/nchstp

i-STD
www.i-std.com

SUMMER CAMPS FOR CHILDREN

GLBT friendly summer camps
www.hrc.org/familynet

SUPPORT

Gay and Lesbian National Hot Line
888-THE-GLNH (843-4564)

Gay and Lesbian Political Action and Support Groups
www.gaypasg.org

National Gay and Lesbian Community Centers
www.lgbtcenters.org

OutProud: Suppport for GBLT youth
www.outproud.org

Pridenet
www.pridenet.com

SUPPORT FOR PARENTS AND FRIENDS OF GAYS AND LESBIANS
www.pflag.org

SURROGACY

www.growinggenerations.com

www.surrogacy.com

THERAPISTS

Gay and Lesbian International Therapist Search Engine
www.glitse.com

Gay and Lesbian National Hotline
THE-888-GLNH

Wildflower Resource Network
www.wrnetwork.net

TRANSGENDER (TG)

Employment Issues
www.gendersanity.com

Transgender Forum
www.tgforum.com

Female to Male Transgender Information:
www.ftm-intl.org

Harry Benjamin International Gender Dysphoria Association, Inc
www.hbigda.org

It's Time America
www.tgender.net/ita (national grassroots organization)

List of therapists for TGs
www.drbecky.com/therapists.html

Local TG support groups
www.tgfmall.com

National Transgender Advocacy Coalition
www.ntac.org

Resources for transsexual women
www.annelawrence.com

State by State resource for changing birth certificates
www.drbecky.com/birthcert.html

Transgender Aging Network
www.forge-forward.org/TAN

Transgender at Work Project
www.tgender.net/taw

Transgender Forum Community Center
www.transgender.org

Transgender Guide
www.tgguide.com

Transgender Law and Policy Institute
www.transgenderlaw.org

www.transgenesis.org

www.susans.org

www.thetransitionalmale.com

VERMONT CIVIL UNIONS

Banking, Tax and Insurance Law Regarding
Civil Unions in Vermont
www.bishca.state.vt.us/consumpubs/civiluguideweb.htm

Online Vermont Civil Union application
http://bennington.com/government/permits/civilunions.pdf

Vermont Guide to Civil Unions
www.sec.state.vt.us/otherprg/civilunions

VETERANS

American Veterans for Equal Rights (AVER)
www.glbva.org

–Appendix F–
BLANK FORMS

The following forms are samples to guide you. It is always a good idea to save a blank original of each form in case you need it again or in case you make a mistake.

Official government forms can be obtained from the appropriate office and can also be found on the Internet.

Note that some forms contain space for a notary signature. You can have forms notarized at your local bank, an attorney, or a notary public.

Table of Forms

DOMESTIC PARTNERSHIP AGREEMENT

On _____ (date) _____ and _____ agree to
the following:

1. We are both over 18 years of age.

2. We are both mentally competent.

3. Neither party is married or part of another domestic partnership agreement.

4. We have chosen to enter into a domestic partnership arrangement in which we will share our lives and our residence.

5. All property owned by each of us prior to entering this agreement will continue to be owned separately.

6. Any property received as a gift or inherited during our domestic partnership will be solely owned by the person receiving it.

7. Any real property owned by the individual parties will continue to be held separately.

8. Income earned or property jointly acquired during the course of our domestic partnership will be owned by the parties jointly.

9. Debt that is jointly incurred during the course of the partnership shall be owed equally by both parties.

10. Debt that is individually incurred during the course of the partnership shall be the sole responsibility of the party incurring it, but can be paid for out of joint earnings if both parties agree.

11. If the parties separate and end their domestic partnership, each shall continue to own all property he or she came into the partnership with and will continue to own any property received as a gift or inheritance during the term of the partnership. Property that is jointly owned shall be divided equally between the parties.

12. The parties agree to use a mediator if they are unable to agree upon how property should be divided.

13. This agreement may be terminated with two weeks written notice.

14. If any part of this agreement is determined to be unenforceable or illegal, that portion shall be severable and the rest of the agreement will be enforced.

This represents the parties' complete understandings and agreements. No other promises, agreements or representations have been made outside the scope of this agreement.

This agreement shall be governed by the laws of the state of

_____ .

_____   _____   _____
name   signed   date

_____   _____   _____
name   signed   date

Notary:

DOMESTIC PARTNERSHIP VERSION FOR EMPLOYER

This agreement is made on _____ (date) between
_____ and _____.

    1. The parties assert that both are over the age of 18 and are not related to each other by blood.

    2. The parties assert that neither is married or engaged in any other domestic partnership agreement.

    3. The parties assert that both are mentally capable and competent.

    4. The parties assert that they are domestic partners to each other and have been since _____ (date).

    5. The parties assert that they live together and support each other.

    6. The parties assert that they intend to remain together as domestic partners.

    7. We agree to notify the person/entity to whom this notice is being submitted if there is a change pertaining to it.

_____   _____   _____
name   signature   date

_____   _____   _____
name   signature   date

Notary:

ROOMMATE AGREEMENT

1.   This agreement is made on _____ (date) by _____ (Tenant) and _____ (Roommate).

2.   Tenant and Roommate agree to share the premises located at _____ for the period beginning _____ and ending _____, during which time Tenant has a valid lease for the premises.

3.   Roommate shall pay $_____ to Tenant per month, for rent/utilities OR Roommate shall pay $_____ per month for rent and shall pay _____% of utility bills per month. Payment is due on the _____ day of each month. Roommate shall be responsible as follows for telephone bills :_____ _____.

4.   Should Roommate fail to pay the rent due, Tenant may serve Roommate with a Three Day Termination Notice. Roommate will vacate the premises in the time specified in the Notice, but will remain liable to Tenant under the terms of this agreement.

5.   Roommate agrees that this agreement covers the use of the following rooms/areas by Roommate: _____ _____.

6.   Roommate has read the original lease (attached) and agrees to all of the terms and restrictions contained in it.

7.   The parties agree that Roommate shall be responsible for the following jobs/chores/items: _____ _____. and that Tenant shall be responsible for the following jobs/chores/items:_____

8.   Roommate also agrees to the following requirements and/or restrictions:_____ _____.

9.   The parties agree that either Roommate or Tenant may end this agreement with one month's written notice to the other party.

10.   Roommate does not have the right to assign this agreement to a third party or to sublet any part of the premises. Roommate has no right to a renewal lease for the premises from Landlord.

11.   Tenant remains responsible to the Landlord for the terms of the original lease, but Roommate is responsible for any damage to the premises caused by Roommate and is subject to eviction and liability.

_____   _____
(Tenant signature)   Date

_____   _____
(Roommate signature)   Date

NOTIFICATION OF ROOMMATE

To: _____ (landlord)

_____

_____

Please be advised that _____ is now
my rommate for the unit located at:

_____

_____

_____ (tenant) _____ (date)

_____ (address)

_____

HOSPITAL VISITATION AUTHORIZATION

I _____ hereby make this authorization form of my own free will.

    1. I reside at _____.

    2. In the event that I am hospitalized in any hospital, medical facility, a nursing home or rehabilitative care facility I authorize _____ to have first priority to visit me and spend time with me while I am in the facility.

    3. This authorization is made in addition to / instead of authorization for any other parties related to me.

I reserve the right to give different instructions once I am conscious and able to communicate.

_____   _____ _____

name   signature   date

Notary:

SAMPLE PARENTING PLAN

_____ (parent A) and _____ (parent B) make this agreement with regard to their parenting time with the child/children _____.

1. The parties agree that they will share joint legal custody of the child/children and will share their access time as specified in this agreement.

2. The parties agree that the child/children will live primarily with parent A, but that both parents are committed to sharing their time with the child/children.

3. Parent B shall spend time with the child/children on alternate weekends from Friday at 5:30 pm to Sunday at 4 pm and every Wednesday from 4 pm to 7:30 pm.

4. Parent B shall spend other time with the child/children at other times as agreed upon by the parties.

5. The parties agree to alternate the following holidays on a yearly basis: New Year's Day, Easter/Passover, Memorial Day, Fourth of July, Labor Day, Thanksgiving, the day after Thanksgiving, Christmas Eve/Hanukah and Christmas Day/Hanukah dates as agreed.

6. The parties agree to alternate the child's/children's birthday(s) yearly.

7. Parent B shall have two uninterrupted weeks of time with the child over summer vacation and four uninterrupted days of time with the child over Easter/spring break. These vacation times will be in addition to regularly scheduled access time.

8. The parties agree that the child/children shall have telephone/email access with the opposite parent from whichever home he/she/they is/are at.

9. The parties agree not to argue in front of the child/children and instead to discuss parenting and scheduling issues either by phone or in a private meeting.

10. The parties agree that both shall have equal access to the child's/chiuldren's school and health care records.

11. The parties agree to give each other the right of first refusal when a babysitter is needed.

12. The parties agree that the children should be permitted to continue with his/her/their extracurricular activities as much as possible. The parent the child is with at the time will have the responsibility of transporting the child to and from scheduled events. Each parent has the discretion to choose to cancel an event scheduled during his or her time, but agree to do so only when necessary.

13. Parent B will pick up the child for scheduled access times but will not come into Parent A's residence unless invited by Parent A.

14. The parties agree not to take the child out of the continental U.S. without the permission of the other parent.

15. The parties agree that the child will be responsible for packing his/her own belongings to take on access time. He or she is responsible for his or her own laundry.

16. The parties agree to consult each other about curfews for the child.

17. The parties agree the child is not old enough to be left without adult supervision.

18. The parties agree neither will drink alcohol, smoke cigarettes or use drugs in the presence of the child.

19. The parties agree to make reasonable and necessary changes to this agreement and agree to give each other as much notice as possible of scheduling changes.

_____   _____

signed   date

_____   _____

signed   date

ORGAN DONATION WISHES

I, _____, hereby create this document to give my consent for organ donation. I agree that any and all parts of my body may be used for transplant by authorized medical personnel after my death. I name _____ as my agent who may consent on my behalf in place of next of kin.

_____   _____   _____

name   signature   date

Notary:

DIVISION OF PROPERTY LIST

Items that were mine before partnership:

_____

_____

_____

_____

_____

_____

_____

_____

_____

Items that were your before partnership:

_____

_____

_____

_____

_____

_____

_____

_____

Items obtained during partnership that are mine:

_____

_____

_____

_____

_____

_____

_____

_____

Items obtained during the partnership that are yours:

_____

_____

_____

_____

_____

_____

_____

_____

_____

_____

_____

Joint Property:

Description	Mine	Yours

CONSENT TO OBTAIN MEDICAL TREATMENT FOR MINOR CHILD

I, _____, am the legal parent of the child
_____. I give my consent for _____, my
child's stepparent to obtain health care for my child and to make
any and all decisions necessary at the time, upon the advice of a
licensed medical care provider. This includes but is not limited to
making decisions about emergency care, routine care, surgery, tests,
x-rays, hospitalization, dental care, mental health care, physical therapy and medications.

_____   _____
signed   date

Notary:

INSEMINATION AGREEMENT

This agreement is made on _____ (date) between the parties _____ (the donor) and _____ (the recipient).

1. The parties are both single and never married.

2. The donor agrees to provide semen to the recipient for use in artificial insemination.

3. The parties agree that the semen may be frozen and saved for future use and may also be used immediately.

4. The recipient agrees to pay the donor $_____ for each semen donation he makes under the terms of this agreement.

5. The parties agree that the donor is making donations for use by the recipient in her attempts to become pregnant. The recipient plans to use artificial insemination of the donor's semen during the following time period _____ to become pregnant.

6. The donor is donating semen for the recipient's use and agrees not to seek custody, visitation, guardianship or contact with any child that results from the insemination. He hereby waives any and all parental rights now or in the future and waives any right as to the names of the children resulting from the insemination.

7. The donor agrees that she has no right to seek financial assistance from the donor and waives all rights to child support, confinement expenses or birth expenses for herself or any resulting child.

8. Both parties agree not to seek a determination of paternity of any child resulting from the insemination in any court or tribunal and waive any right to any such determination of paternity.

9. The parties agree that the birth certificates for any children resulting from the insemination will not name a father and specifically will not name the donor in any capacity.

10. The parties agree to use a licensed physician to perform the insemination. This is in compliance with _____ (fill in state law if applicable) to avoid the donor being named as the legal father of the child.

initial: _____   _____

11. The identity of the donor will be kept secret by both the donor and recipient and will not be revealed with consent of the other party.

12. The recipient shall have the right to choose a guardian for any children resulting from the insemination. The recipient shall also have the right to consent to a second parent adoption of any children resulting from the insemination. Donor shall in no way interfere with any of these procedures, determinations or exercises of rights.

13. The parties agree that the termination of rights stated in this agreement are permanent and irrevocable. Neither party may institute any court proceeding involving custody, visitation, guardianship, paternity or child support against the other with respect to the children resulting from the insemination.

14. Donor agrees not to have any contact with any children resulting from the insemination without the express knowing consent of the recipient. The parties agree that any contact between donor and the resulting children shall in no way alter, impact or effect the terms of this agreement or the legal relationship of the parties. Any contact that may occur will in no way be seen as implying or allowing donor the right to obtain, seek or ask for parental rights or responsibilities.

15. The parties make this agreement willingly and freely, under no duress. Both parties have been advised to seek separate legal counsel before executing this document.

16. The parties understand each and every provision of this agreement. The agreement contains the entire agreement made between the parties and there are no other promises, understandings or agreements between the parties other than what is contained herein.

17. The numbered provisions of this agreement may be enforced separately and individually by both parties.

18. This agreement is made pursuant to the laws of _____ (your state) and will be enforced according to the laws of that state.

initial: _____   _____

19. The parties agree that this agreement can only be altered in writing and must be signed by both parties to become valid.

_____   _____   _____
Donor Name   Donor Signature   Date

_____   _____   _____
Recipient Name   Recipient Signature   Date

Notary:

BODY DISPOSITION FORM

I, _____, hereby leave the following directions with regard to the disposition of body after my death.

(check all that apply)

_____ I authorize _____as my agent to make all arrangements having to do with my remains, funeral, burial and/or cremation.

_____ I direct my agent to follow funeral or memorial service instructions as follows:_____

_____

_____

_____

(make note of any contracts you have with funeral homes)

_____ I agree that an autopsy may be performed on my body after my death and ask my agent to consent.

_____ I do not authorize my agent to consent to an autopsy.

_____ I authorize my agent to donate any and all parts of my body for organ donation.

_____ I authorize my agent to donate my body or parts of my body to be used for medical research and study.

_____ I direct my agent to bury my remains at the site of his or her choosing

_____ I direct my agent to bury my remains at _____ (indicate if you have a contract with a cemetery)

_____I direct my agent to cremate my remains and dispose of the ashes as he or she chooses.

_____I direct my agent to cremate my remains and dispose of them as follows:_____.

_____   _____   _____

name   signature   date

Notary:

California Domestic Partnership Forms

NOTICE TO POTENTIAL DOMESTIC PARTNER REGISTRANTS

As of July 1, 2003, California's law of intestate succession will change. The intestate succession law specifies what happens to a person's property when that person dies without a will, trust, or other estate plan.

Under the law prior to July 1, 2003, if a domestic partner dies without a will, trust, or other estate plan, a surviving domestic partner cannot inherit any of the deceased partner's separate property. Instead, surviving relatives, including, for example, children, brothers, sisters, nieces, nephews, or parents may inherit the deceased partner's separate property.

Under the law to take effect July 1, 2003, if a domestic partner dies without a will, trust, or other estate plan, the surviving domestic partner will inherit the deceased partner's separate property in the same manner as a surviving spouse. This change will mean that the surviving domestic partner would inherit a third, a half, or all of the deceased partner's separate property, depending on whether the deceased domestic partner has surviving children or other relatives. This change does not affect any community or quasi-community property that the deceased partner may have had.

This change in the intestate succession law will not affect you if you have a will, trust, or other estate plan.

If you do not have a will, trust, or other estate plan and you do not wish to have your domestic partner inherit your separate property in the manner provided by the revised law, you may prepare a will, trust, or other estate plan, or terminate your domestic partnership.

Under existing law, your domestic partnership is automatically terminated if you or your partner married or died while you were registered as domestic partners. It is also terminated by you sending your partner or your partner sending to you by certified mail a notice terminating the domestic partnership, or by you and your partner no longer sharing a common residence. In all cases, you are required to file a Notice of Termination of Domestic Partnership with the Secretary of State in order to establish the actual date of termination of the domestic partnership. You can obtain a Notice of Termination of Domestic Partnership from the Secretary of State's office.

If your domestic partnership has terminated because you sent your partner or your partner sent to you a notice of termination of your domestic partnership, you must immediately file a Notice of Termination of Domestic Partnership. If you do not file that notice, your former domestic partner may inherit under the new law. However, if your domestic partnership has terminated because you or your partner married or you and your partner no longer share a common residence, neither you nor your former partner may inherit from the other under this new law.

If you have any questions about this change, please consult an estate planning attorney. If you cannot find an estate planning attorney in your locale, please contact your county bar association for a referral.

State of California
Kevin Shelley
Secretary of State

FILE NO: _____

DECLARATION OF DOMESTIC PARTNERSHIP
(Family Code Section 298)

Instructions:

1. Complete and mail to: Secretary of State, P.O. Box 942877, Sacramento, CA 94277-0001 (916) 653-4984
2. Include filing fee of $10.00. Make check payable to Secretary of State.

We the undersigned, do declare that we meet the requirements of Section 297 at this time:

(Office Use Only)

We share a common residence;
We agree to be jointly responsible for each other's basic living expenses incurred during our domestic partnership;
Neither of us is married or a member of another domestic partnership;
We are not related by blood in a way that would prevent us from being married to each other in this state;
We are both at least 18 years of age;
We are both members of the same sex or one/or both of us is/are over the age of 62 and meet the eligibility criteria under Title II of the Social Security Act as defined in 42 U.S.C. Section 402(a) for old-age insurance benefits or Title XVI of the Social Security Act as defined in 42 U.S.C Section 1381 for aged individuals;
We are both capable of consenting to the domestic partnership;
Neither of us has previously filed a Declaration of Domestic Partnership with the Secretary of State pursuant to Division 2.5 of the Family Code that has not been terminated under Section 299 of the Family Code.

The representations herein are true, correct and contain no material omissions of fact to our best knowledge and belief. Sign and print complete name. (If not printed legibly, application will be rejected.) **Signatures of both partners must be notarized.**

Signature	(Last)	(First)	(Middle)
Signature	(Last)	(First)	(Middle)
Common Residence Address	City	State	Zip Code
Mailing Address	City	State	Zip Code

NOTARIZATION IS REQUIRED
State of California
County of _____

On _____, before me, _____, personally

appeared _____
personally known to me (or proved to me on the basis of satisfactory evidence) to be the person(s) whose name(s) is/are subscribed to the within instrument and acknowledged to me that he/she/they executed the same in his/her/their authorized capacity(ies), and that by his/her/their signature(s) on the instrument the person(s) executed the instrument.

Signature of Notary Public

[PLACE NOTARY SEAL HERE]

SEC/STATE LP/SF DP-1 (Rev 01/2003)

State of California
Kevin Shelley
Secretary of State

FILE NO: _____

(Office Use Only)

NOTICE OF TERMINATION OF DOMESTIC PARTNERSHIP
(Family Code Section 299)

Instructions:

1. Complete and send by **CERTIFIED** mail to:
    Secretary of State
    P.O. Box 942877
    Sacramento, CA 94277-0001
    (916) 653-4984

2. **There is no fee for filing this Notice of Termination**

I, the undersigned, do declare that:

Former Partner: _____ and I are no longer Domestic Partners.
            (Last)   (First)   (Middle)

Secretary of State File Number: _____.

If termination is caused by death or marriage of the domestic partner please indicate the date of the death or the
marriage: _____.
            (month/day/year)

This date shall be the actual termination date for the Domestic Partnership as provided in Family Code Section
299.

_____   _____   _____   _____
Signature   (Last)   (First)   (Middle)

_____   _____   _____   _____
Mailing Address   City   State   Zip Code

NOTARIZATION IS REQUIRED
State of California
County of _____

On _____, before me, _____, personally appeared

_____

personally known to me (or proved to me on the basis of satisfactory evidence) to be the person whose name is subscribed to the
within instrument and acknowledged to me that he/she executed the same in his/her authorized capacity, and that by his/her
signature on the instrument the person executed the instrument.

_____
Signature of Notary Public   [PLACE NOTARY SEAL HERE]

SEC/STATE LP/SF DP-2 (Dec 1999)

VERMONT DEPARTMENT OF HEALTH
APPLICATION FOR VERMONT LICENSE OF CIVIL UNION
FEE FOR CIVIL UNION LICENSE: $23
COST OF CERTIFIED COPY: $7

PARTY A

1. NAME (First, Middle, Last)		1b. MAIDEN NAME (If Applicable)	1c. DATE OF BIRTH (Month, Day, Year)

2. SEX	3. MAILING ADDRESS (Street and Number or Rural Route Number, City or Town, Zip Code)		

4a. USUAL RESIDENCE - STATE	4b. CITY OR TOWN		5. BIRTHPLACE (State or Foreign Country)

6a. FATHER'S NAME (First, Middle, Last)	6b. BIRTHPLACE (State or Foreign Country)	7a. MOTHER'S NAME (First, Middle, Maiden Surname)	7b. BIRTHPLACE (State or Foreign Country)

PARTY B

8. NAME (First, Middle, Last)		8b. MAIDEN NAME (If Applicable)	

9. SEX	10. MAILING ADDRESS (Street and Number or Rural Route Number, City or Town, Zip Code)		

11a. USUAL RESIDENCE - STATE	11b. CITY OR TOWN		12. BIRTHPLACE (State or Foreign Country)

13a. FATHER'S NAME (First, Middle, Last)	13b. BIRTHPLACE (State or Foreign Country)	14a. MOTHER'S NAME (First, Middle, Maiden Surname)	14b. BIRTHPLACE (State or Foreign Country)

THE INFORMATION BELOW IS CONFIDENTIAL AND WILL NOT APPEAR ON CERTIFIED COPIES OF THE RECORD.

PARTY A

20. NAME		IF PREVIOUSLY MARRIED OR IN A CIVIL UNION			EDUCATION (Specify only highest grade completed)	
		LAST MARRIAGE OR CIVIL UNION ENDED BY		DATE	Elementary or Secondary (0-12)	College (1-4 or 5+)
21. RACE – White, Black, American Indian, etc. (Specify)	22. TOTAL NO. OF CIVIL UNIONS OR MARRIAGES INCLUDING THIS ONE	DEATH DIVORCE	DISSOLUTION ANNULMENT	MONTH YEAR		
		23a.		23b.	24.	

PARTY B

20. NAME		IF PREVIOUSLY MARRIED OR IN A CIVIL UNION			EDUCATION (Specify only highest grade completed)	
		LAST MARRIAGE OR CIVIL UNION ENDED BY		DATE	Elementary or Secondary (0-12)	College (1-4 or 5+)
21. RACE – White, Black, American Indian, etc. (Specify)	22. TOTAL NO. OF CIVIL UNIONS OR MARRIAGES INCLUDING THIS ONE	DEATH DIVORCE	DISSOLUTION ANNULMENT	MONTH YEAR		
		23a.		23b.	24.	

DOES EITHER PARTY HAVE A LEGAL GUARDIAN? ___ YES ___ NO

APPLICANTS

We hereby certify that the information provided is correct to the best of our knowledge and belief and that we are free to form a civil union under the laws of the State of Vermont.

15a. SIGNATURE	15b. DATE SIGNED	16a. SIGNATURE	16b. DATE SIGNED

Planned date of certification _____ Location (City or Town) _____

Officiant Name & Address _____

Your mailing address after certification _____

Do you want a certified copy of your Civil Union Certificate? ($7.00) ___ Yes ___ No

Date License Issued _____ Clerk Issuing License _____

THIS WORKSHEET MAY BE DESTROYED AFTER CIVIL UNION REGISTERED

SOCIAL SECURITY ADMINISTRATION
Application for a Social Security Card

Form Approved
OMB No. 0960-0066

1	**NAME** TO BE SHOWN ON CARD	First	Full Middle Name	Last
	FULL NAME AT BIRTH IF OTHER THAN ABOVE	First	Full Middle Name	Last
	OTHER NAMES USED			

2 **MAILING ADDRESS** Do Not Abbreviate
Street Address, Apt. No., PO Box, Rural Route No.

City — State — Zip Code

3 **CITIZENSHIP** (Check One) — ☐ U.S. Citizen ☐ Legal Alien Allowed To Work ☐ Legal Alien Not Allowed To Work (See Instructions On Page 1) ☐ Other (See Instructions On Page 1)

4 **SEX** — ☐ Male ☐ Female

5 **RACE/ETHNIC DESCRIPTION** (Check One Only - Voluntary) — ☐ Asian, Asian-American or Pacific Islander ☐ Hispanic ☐ Black (Not Hispanic) ☐ North American Indian or Alaskan Native ☐ White (Not Hispanic)

6 **DATE OF BIRTH** Month, Day, Year

7 **PLACE OF BIRTH** (Do Not Abbreviate) City — State or Foreign Country — FCI   Office Use Only

8	**A. MOTHER'S MAIDEN NAME**	First	Full Middle Name	Last Name At Her Birth
	B. MOTHER'S SOCIAL SECURITY NUMBER → ☐☐☐ – ☐☐ – ☐☐☐☐			

9	**A. FATHER'S NAME** →	First	Full Middle Name	Last
	B. FATHER'S SOCIAL SECURITY NUMBER → ☐☐☐ – ☐☐ – ☐☐☐☐			

10 Has the applicant or anyone acting on his/her behalf ever filed for or received a Social Security number card before?
☐ Yes (If "yes", answer questions 11-13.)   ☐ No (If "no", go on to question 14.)   ☐ Don't Know (If "don't know", go on to question 14.)

11 Enter the Social Security number previously assigned to the person listed in item 1. → ☐☐☐ – ☐☐ – ☐☐☐☐

12 Enter the name shown on the most recent Social Security card issued for the person listed in item 1. → First   Middle Name   Last

13 Enter any different date of birth if used on an earlier application for a card. → Month, Day, Year

14 **TODAY'S DATE** Month, Day, Year

15 **DAYTIME PHONE NUMBER** ( ) Area Code   Number

I declare under penalty of perjury that I have examined all the information on this form, and on any accompanying statements or forms, and it is true and correct to the best of my knowledge.

16 ► **YOUR SIGNATURE**

17 **YOUR RELATIONSHIP TO THE PERSON IN ITEM 1 IS:** ☐ Self ☐ Natural Or Adoptive Parent ☐ Legal Guardian ☐ Other (Specify)

DO NOT WRITE BELOW THIS LINE (FOR SSA USE ONLY)

NPN			DOC	NTI	CAN		ITV
PBC	EVI	EVA	EVC	PRA	NWR	DNR	UNIT
EVIDENCE SUBMITTED					SIGNATURE AND TITLE OF EMPLOYEE(S) REVIEWING EVIDENCE AND/OR CONDUCTING INTERVIEW		
							DATE
					DCL		DATE

Form SS-5 (3-2001)   EF (07-2002)   Destroy Prior Editions   Page 5

U.S. Department of State

U.S. PASSPORT AMENDMENT/VALIDATION APPLICATION
(SEE INSTRUCTIONS ON REVERSE)
TYPE OR PRINT IN INK IN WHITE AREAS ONLY

IDENTIFYING INFORMATION

NAME   FIRST NAME   MIDDLE NAME

LAST NAME   SOCIAL SECURITY NUMBER

MAILING ADDRESS

STREET   HOME PHONE

CITY, STATE, ZIP CODE   (Area Code)
                                                             BUSINESS PHONE

IN CARE OF
                                                             (Area Code)

SEX   PLACE OF BIRTH   DATE OF BIRTH   DEPARTURE DATE

☐ ☐
Male Female   City, State or Province, Country   (mm-dd-yyyy)   (mm-dd-yyyy)

U.S. PASSPORT NUMBER   ISSUE DATE   PLACE OF ISSUE   DOCUMENT CODE

                                                                    A

                        (mm-dd-yyyy)   (For Official Use Only)
                        PERMANENT ADDRESS (Street, City, State, ZIP Code)

NAME CHANGE (Submit original or certified document)

CHANGE NAME TO READ AS FOLLOWS: NAME CURRENTLY IN PASSPORT

                    DATE OF MARRIAGE   SPOUSE'S NAME IN FULL

NAME CHANGED BY MARRIAGE
                    (mm-dd-yyyy)

                    NAME OF COURT   LOCATION (City, State)   DATE

NAME CHANGED
BY COURT ORDER
                                                                    (mm-dd-yyyy)

                                OTHER (Specify)

OTHER ACTION REQUESTED

OATH AND SIGNATURE I have not since acquiring United States citizenship, performed any of the acts listed under "Acts or Conditions" on this application form (unless explanatory statement is attached). I solemnly swear (or affirm) that the statements made on this application are true.

FOR PASSPORT SERVICES USE ONLY

            X

Date (mm-dd-yyyy)   Signature of Applicant

☐ Evidence _____
☐ Name Change   ☐ Extend To _____
☐ Add Visa Pages   ☐ Endorsement No. _____
☐ Rewrite _____   ☐ Limit To _____
☐ Other: _____   ☐ Void limitation on page _____

        Examiner's Name   Office, Date

DS-19
12-2002   OMB No. 1405-0007 Expires: 12\31\2005 Estimated Burden 5 Minutes (See Page 2)   Page 1 of 2

U.S. Department of State

U.S. PASSPORT AMENDMENT/VALIDATION APPLICATION

YOU MAY REQUEST AMENDMENT/VALIDATION OF YOUR PASSPORT FOR THE FOLLOWING REASONS ONLY:

- TO SHOW A CHANGE OF NAME. Submit documentary evidence such as a certified court order, marriage certificate, or other satisfactory evidence to support a change of name.
- TO CORRECT THE DESCRIPTIVE DATA. Submit appropriate evidence to support correction of descriptive data.
- TO ADD VISA SUPPLEMENT PAGES.
- TO EXTEND THE VALIDITY OF A LIMITED U.S. PASSPORT. Submit appropriate evidence to support your request.
- IN CERTAIN CASES, TO SHOW ENDORSEMENT OR VALIDATION OF YOUR U.S. PASSPORT. Submit appropriate evidence.

HOW TO APPLY FOR AMENDMENT/VALIDATION OF YOUR U.S. PASSPORT

- COMPLETE, SIGN, and DATE this passport amendment/validation application.
- SEND it with your U.S. passport and any required additional evidence to:

    Charleston Passport Center
    Attn: Amendments
    1269 Holland Street
    Charleston, SC 29405

- THERE IS NO FEE TO HAVE A U.S. PASSPORT AMENDED. Your amended U.S. passport and any documentary evidence submitted will be returned to you by first-class mail.
- For faster processing, you may request Expedited Service. Expedite requests will be processed in three workdays from receipt at the Passport Center. The fee for expedited service is $60. Enclose the $60 expedite fee in the form of a personal check or money order. All fees should be payable to the "U.S. DEPARTMENT OF STATE." Do not send cash. Expedited Service is available only in the United States.
- If you desire SPECIAL POSTAL SERVICE (overnight mail, special delivery, etc.), include appropriate postage fees or a pre-paid envelope. NOTE: The Passport Center will NOT mail a passport to a private address outside the United States.

NOTICE TO APPLICANTS FOR AMENDMENT/VALIDATION OF OFFICIAL, DIPLOMATIC, OR NO-FEE PASSPORTS
    Submit your U.S. Government or military authorization in addition to the items listed above. Consult your sponsoring Agency for instructions on proper routing procedures before forwarding this application. Your amended/validated passport will be released to your sponsoring Agency for forwarding to you.

ATTENTION: IF THERE IS AN ERROR IN THE DESCRIPTIVE DATA OF YOUR RECENTLY ISSUED PASSPORT, PLEASE FORWARD YOUR REQUEST TO THE RESPECTIVE ISSUING AGENCY

FEDERAL TAX LAW

26 U.S.C. 6039E (Internal Revenue Code) requires a passport applicant to provide his or her name and social security number. If you have not been issued a social security number, enter zeros in the designated box. The U.S. Department of State must provide this information to the Internal Revenue Service routinely. Any applicant who fails to provide the required information is subject to a $500 penalty enforced by the IRS. All questions on this matter should be referred to the nearest IRS office.

ACTS OR CONDITIONS

(If any of the below-mentioned acts or conditions has been performed by or apply to the applicant, the portion which applies should be lined out, and a supplementary explanatory statement under oath (or affirmation) by the applicant should be attached and made a part of this application.) I have not, since acquiring United States citizenship, been naturalized as a citizen of a foreign state; taken an oath or made an affirmation or other formal declaration of allegiance to a foreign state; entered or served in the armed forces of a foreign state; accepted or performed the duties of any office, post, or employment under the government of a foreign state or political subdivision thereof; made a formal renunciation of nationality either in the United States, or before a diplomatic or consular officer of the United States in a foreign state; or been convicted by a court or court martial of competent jurisdiction of committing any act of treason against, or attempting by force to overthrow, put down, or to destroy by force, the Government of the United States.

WARNING: False statements made knowingly and willfully in passport applications or in affidavits or other supporting documents submitted therewith are punishable by fine and/or imprisonment under provisions of 18 U.S.C. 1001 and/or 18 U.S.C. 1542. Alteration or mutilation of a passport issued pursuant to this application is punishable by fine and/or imprisonment under the provisions of 18 U.S.C. 1543. The use of a passport in violation of the restrictions contained therein or of the passport regulations is punishable by fine and/or imprisonment under 18 U.S.C. 1544. All statements and documents submitted are subject to verification.

PRIVACY ACT AND PAPERWORK REDUCTION ACT STATEMENTS

AUTHORITIES: The information solicited on this form is requested pursuant to provisions in Titles 8, 18, and 22 of the United States Code, whether or not codified, including specifically 22 U.S.C. 211a, 212, and 213, and all regulations issued pursuant to Executive Order 11295 (August 5, 1966), including Part 51, Title 22, Code of Federal Regulations (CFR). Also, as specifically noted, pursuant to 26 U.S.C. 6039E.

PURPOSE: The primary purpose for soliciting the information is to establish citizenship, identity, and entitlement to issuance of a U.S. passport. The information may also be used in connection with issuing other travel documents or evidence of citizenship, and in furtherance of the Secretary's responsibility for the protection of U.S. nationals abroad.

ROUTINE USES: The information solicited on this form may be made available as a routine use to other government agencies, to assist the U.S. Department of State in adjudicating passport applications, and for law enforcement and administrative purposes. It may also be disclosed pursuant to court order. The information may be made available to foreign government agencies to fulfill passport control and immigration duties or to investigate or prosecute violations of law. The information may be made available to private U.S. citizen 'wardens' designated by U.S. embassies and consulates.

Failure to provide the information requested on this form may also result in the denial of a United States passport, related document, or service to the individual seeking such passport, document, or service.

Public reporting burden for this collection of information is estimated to average 5 minutes per response, including time required for searching existing data sources, gathering the necessary data, providing the information required, and reviewing the final collection. You do not have to provide the information unless this collection displays a currently valid OMB number. Send comments on the accuracy of this estimate of the burden and recommendations for reducing it to: U.S. Department of State (A/RPS/DIR) Washington, DC 20520.

DS-19

INDEX

L

Lambda Legal, 5, 9, 13
landlords, 10, 20, 121
Lavender Phone Book, 3
Lawrence and Garner v. Texas, 2
legal help, 4
  ACLU (American Civil
    Liberties Union), 5
  attorneys, 4
  legal aid office, 5
Lesbian and Gay Immigration
  Rights Task Force, 58
Lesbian Community Cancer
  Project, 41
liability insurance, 57
life insurance, 31, 54
  guaranteed insurability rider, 55
  HIV, 56
  Medical Information Bureau
    (MIB), 55
  viatical settlements, 41
limited liability companies (LLCs),
  54, 66
living trusts, 35, 94
  estate planning, 94
  wills, 94
living wills, 43
  health care provider liability, 44
  revoking, 45
Local Law Enforcement
  Enhancement Act , 16
Lofton v. Kearny, 102
long-term care insurance, 39
Louisiana
  birth father registries, 102
  hate crime laws, 15
  same-sex second parent adop-
    tions, 101
  sodomy, 2

M

Maine
  hate crime laws, 15
maintenance. *See alimony*
marriage, 129
  divorce. *See divorce*
  transgenders, 129
Marvin v. Marvin, 126
Mary-Helen Mautner Project for
  Lesbians with Cancer, 41
Maryland
  employment discrimination pro-
    tection, 12
  hate crime laws, 16
  housing discrimination protec-
    tion, 10
  same-sex second parent adop-
    tions, 101
Massachusetts
  credit discrimination protection,
    11
  employment discrimination pro-
    tection, 12
  gender identity discrimination
    protection, 90
  hate crime laws, 15
  housing discrimination protec-
    tion, 10
  psychological parents, 97
  Safe School Laws, 14
  Safe Schools Program, 115
  same-sex second parent adop-
    tions, 101
Matthew Shepard, 15
mediation, 116, 123, 126, 130, 131
Medicaid, 40
  gay penalty, 40
medical decision making
  do not resuscitate orders, 45
  emergency contact cards, 41
  end of life issues, 48

ABOUT THE AUTHOR

Brette McWhorter Sember earned her JD from the State University of New York at Buffalo and practiced law before becoming a writer. Her general practice focused on individual's and families' rights and also included mediation. In her practice, Sember volunteered her time to provide community mediation services through the Better Business Bureau, represented children in family and matrimonial cases through the Law Guardian program and served as a volunteer attorney, accepting clients who could not afford legal services through the Volunteer Lawyers Project. Her contact with clients, as well as her experience in mediating problems, made it clear to her that there are many situations in which the law does not provide protection, assistance, or clear answers for the real and important needs and problems people face. The GLBT community is one of those groups left out in the cold most often.

Recently, Sember worked closely with the development of a GLBT phone book. Sember is the author of nine other Sphinx titles dealing with divorce, custody, visitation, credit, real estate and business. She is also the author of a children's book and writes often about issues affecting parents, children and families. Visit her website at:

www.MooseintheBirdbath.com